Prologue

was 10 years of age then, at that point. It more likely than not been a day in Summer 1998. 'Father, for what reason do you go to the Union Office and pay them each month?'

'It is a training in the Communist Party, child. We laborers should forfeit a piece of our wages so the party survives.'

'So father, you mean your party is poor?' 'Yes.'

'For what reason do you host to have a place with a gathering that is poor? How about you join a rich party, dad?'

'I'm a Unionist. My Union is associated to the Communist faction. Socialist coalitions are the ones in particular which work for poor people and the abused. Rich gatherings don't work for the poor'

'For what reason don't they work for the poor?'

Child, Rich gatherings are rich since they are subsidized by rich individuals. Rich individuals, as a rule need just to become more extravagant. They support ideological groups and make them rich. When the party becomes rich and catches influence it will begin working for them. The patrons thus get more extravagant and they store the rich party more. The cycle proceeds. All gatherings in India are rich gatherings. Just the Communist Party is subsidized by me, Clerk Varada Uncle, Auto Driver Govindan Uncle, Maran Master, Plumber Udhayakumar Uncle, etc. Poor and working class individuals like us are the ones in particular who store this party. Indeed, even Kerala CM is poor'

• • •CieloCielo

Must be ten years after the fact. I was twenty years of age then, at that point. 2008.

'Father, individuals say the entire world is trapped in a downturn, out of nowhere one fine morning. Wasn't there any individual who could anticipate this and stop before it got worse?'

'Only one individual so far has anticipated this and he is as of now

not alive' 'Gracious incredible father, Who?'

'Karl Marx, he anticipated effectively how free enterprise will act. Do you know there is a huge interest for Das Capital composed by him now in Germany, almost 150 years after it was published?

'Father, so do you say Marxism will fix the universe of every one of its

concerns?' 'Without a doubt, son'

For what reason did Russia surrender Communism then?'

A ton of reasons. Individuals were childish and needed to acquire quickly'

'Goodness alright, father. I needed to inquire as to for what reason would you say you are getting back home early these days after office? Such an extremely long time you generally used to come not before 9 PM'

'I'm at this point not dynamic in the Union. I was supplanted in the Union by Suresh, my associate you know'

Gracious. Why?'

Part of infighting. I likewise brought up issues on the Communist Party's methodology towards industrialisation in West Bengal. You caught wind of firings on local people in Singur and Nandigram? I let them know that we will lose West Bengal assuming we proceed with this way. The Unit authority was upset that I talked this way. They chose to supplant me. So I quit being dynamic in the Union and the Party'.

♣ ♣ ♣CieloCielo

It was 2018. My dad had resigned from his job.

Father did you take a gander at the news that main 1% of the populace in India possesses in excess of 60% of India's wealth?'

'Yes. Free enterprise Capitalism works like

that' 'Wasn't India inconsistent like this

before?'

'It wasn't this inconsistent. We accepted financial changes in 1991. So our abundance dispersion began to slant. We have the greater part 1,000,000 ranchers dead because of State Negligence. Our State never again is a Welfare State'

Father, I read some place that the idea of Welfare State emerged in the West. So did India duplicate that?'

'Indeed, the USSR held onto all method for creation from landowners and industrialists. The state controlled everything. Rich individuals in the West were worried about the possibility that that in case Communism spreads to their country, they might need to lose

everything. So they joined components of Soviet Communism with Capitalism and advanced something many refer to as Welfare State. It is likewise called a Mixed Economy. Nehru needed to copy that in India. He did with just moderate success.'

'Father, so you intend to say that the breakdown of the USSR went connected at the hip with the world returning to Laissez Faire Capitalism?'

'Yes. That was one of the key reasons. Once there was no stabilizer to the Free Market West as the USSR, the West begun spreading unrestricted economy thoughts to the Third-World like India. India wouldn't have likely accepted the Free Market had the USSR figured out how to live past 1991'.

♣ ♠ ♠CieloCielo

A year after the fact, 2019. A couple of days before I began composing this book.

'Father, I am part of the way through Pin Thodarum Nizhalin Kural by Jeyamohan. He has blamed Stalin for killing huge number of Russians. For what reason did Stalin do that? Isn't the possibility of Marxism based on affection, similar to how Kamal Haasan accentuated in Anbe Sivam?'

'Don't trust what the bourgeoisie scholars say. They don't know anything'

'Father, he isn't a bourgeoisie. He was once a piece of the Communist Party

himself. You have let me know numerous a period that Communists are straightforward individuals. For what reason does he need to lie?'

'You never know in the Communist Party. There might be awful individuals as well'

And they might be killed too by the actual Party, father?'

'I'm taking a walk. We will talk later'

'Father, I need to realize what truly occurred in the USSR. For what reason was Trotsky killed? Is it safe to say that he wasn't one of the organizers of the USSR? How is it that he could be a terrible individual? For what reason was Bukharin killed?'

You read a lot of George Orwell I presume. This isn't useful for you. Orwell was a traitor'

'Orwell joined the Communist Party however was removed. He lived as a Communist all through his life'

'Individuals leave the party and imagine they are philosophically dedicated' 'Father, who was Pol Pot?'

'He was a Cambodian tyrant. He killed millions'

'He was a Communist, father. How about you notice that?'

'He abused the name of Communism. Be that as it may, he was initially a despot' 'Assuming he was not a Communist, for what reason did Communist China support him in

his battle against Communist Vietnam?'

'You have grown up, child. I have nothing to tell you'

You have to shield your Party. Come on, father. We're simply having a conversation'

'I'm at this point don't part of the Party. I quit when I resigned from administration' 'Gracious what, why dad?'

The Communist Party can't be improved. They are going to doom'

'I don't comprehend. On one issue, you talk like the Party is dependable and any individual who talks against the Party is a deceiver. On another, you say the Party is hopeless. Why there is so much contradiction?'

'I will pass on it to you to track down that, son'.

THE INSTALLATION

CHAPTER I

The Installation

Contrary to what exactly is for the most part accepted, Russia just before the October Revolution was not an all around created modern country. It was not even colonialist, in the Western feeling of the word and had no states in Africa or Asia or Latin America. Russia's looming rout in the First World War towards the finish of 1917, had suppressed all public soul, and a developing number of miscreants in the military hampered even the smallest possibility of a tactical recuperation. The Tsars were set on delaying the battle for their own endurance reasons, yet were stunned to observe rebellions, turmoil and disorder wherever which to a generous degree was the normal reaction to the extremely old cruel and harsh system that they had forced upon their kin. Russia, basically a rural nation had a large number of helpless workers and a little, developing modern low class. The tyrannical Tsar system exposed the laborers to huge tax collection which expanded dramatically with the happening to the World War. Workers frantically trusted that a guardian angel will free them from every unbearable difficulty and certainly placed their faith on a ton of hostile to monarchist developments that were filling to a great extent in Russia.

Revolution Underway:

One such development was going by the Russian Social Democratic Labor Party (RSDLP) which was only a gathering of left wing extremists joined by a wide scope of nineteenth century communist goals. The party had two unmistakable groups which supported different philosophical dreams of a future

idealistic culture however had, luckily chose to determine their disparities at a later place of time - after the defeat of the inflexible Tsarist monarchy.

ne of the groups, the Bolsheviks was going by Vladimir Lenin, a sober minded Marxist, as he jumped at the chance to call himself. The other, the Mensheviks, was going by Alexander Kerensky a communist extremist who didn't endorse Marxism however was, by and by an exceptionally moderate progressive. The Bolsheviks guaranteed ' Land, Peace and Bread' to individuals and consequently had the option to order a wide and an enduring allure among the majority. By mid 1917 as the World War was attracting to a nearby, the Tsar, detecting well known turmoil, surrendered the lofty position which gave way to the establishment of a temporary Government drove by Kerensky. Individuals decided in favor of the RSDLP in general however it was Kerensky who held onto power when he divined its nearness. Kerensky, the politically keen ruler as he was, expecting a reaction from Lenin in the short term, requested for the disposal of the Bolsheviks through legitimate too extra-lawful measures. The power battle followed for quite a long time yet it was uniquely on November 7 that very year that the Bolsheviks held onto power under the authority of the relentless Lenin.

Repercussions:

This takeover of force by Lenin, likewise called the Russian Revolution of 1917 denoted a turning point in the worldwide history of the nineteenth century. This was the initial time ever that an administration transparently embracing Marxist goals was framed in any nation and the shivers it sent through the rest of
the world can't be thought little of. The Imperialist Western Europe was frightened at the climb of the Communists in the biggest nation of the world and without precedent for history the decision classes progressively felt that they needed to defy something 'sceptral' to endure the not so distant future. Then again, the triumph of the Russian Revolution gave desire to a great many persecuted, poor and oppressed individuals in nations world over including provinces like those of India. In each state in Asia and Africa, nearby socialists started to assume the main part in the public freedom battle against the West European Imperialists.

A great deal of European nations alongside the US neglected to perceive the Government of the Soviet Union drove by Lenin which started to fill in size as other connecting nations like Kazakhstan, Armenia, Ukraine, and so forth additionally began agreeing to the Communist Union. Above all the triumph of the Bolsheviks motivated freedom battle in the adjoining China as well,

which was likewise to become Communist in the following 30 years.

Intellectuals all around the world particularly in Great Britain and surprisingly in the US felt that Russia had turned another leaf over and anticipated that their own countries should take action accordingly to achieve a general public without abuse, bigotry and strict enthusiasm. The British Raj in India passed the Rowlatt Act of 1919 prohibiting any type of dissent against the Government to clampdown on the Indian Communists and its supporters. In different settlements, their separate state run administrations restricted their neighborhood Communist coalitions and a monstrous witch-hunting of socialist revolutionaries followed.

The huge land change that the Bolshevik government had attempted in Russia before long its arrangement stripped the aristocrats and sovereigns and property managers of their assets and left them 'cold and threatening to the lowly foundation. They were hanging tight for a chance to take care of Lenin and his cadre, meanwhile hopeless unequivocally for a reclamation of the government. For the ousted Russian decision classes, before long assistance was to show up as Western aid.

The first challenge:

It was 1921 when Lenin's arrangements to resuscitate a conflict assaulted nation were gradually proving to be fruitful, however deficiencies and infrequent starvations happened in the provincial regions. In numerous ways, the work was humongous and Lenin's administration utilized both coercive just as fair means to affect individuals in this noteworthy undertaking. Individuals found huge stores of nationalism and progressive soul inside themselves that they were prepared to serve the Bolshevik government in any way as was required.

However, the ousted controlling classes then again, with generous assistance from the Western powers were carefully plotting for a counter upset dead set on reestablishing Russia to its Tsarist days. Common conflict broke out in 1918 which shocked Lenin and the ridiculous struggle between the Red Army and the counter progressives started to hamper the modifying exertion. The Bolsheviks figured out how to overcome the counter-progressives after a drawn out fight which accidentally wound up adjusting Lenin's mentality towards his kin remarkably.

Lenin under no circumstances, was ready to permit Russia spiral into its pre-1917 period of dimness, because of which his progressive idealism began giving way to an over-wariness that was soon to change into a horrible suspicion. Lenin advanced something that should have been called 'War Communism' which implied a great deal of things including disposal of internal party democracy

and heartless concealment of contradiction. The right to speak freely of discourse and other essential opportunities were to be suspended 'for some time', during which the progressive government will prevail with regards to devastating any enduring relic of 'counter-upset and response' that may conceivably hurt the country's 'noteworthy walk into communism'. Worker's organizations were viably debilitated and the State chose to interrupt into each part of its resident's life in order to cleanse any traditionalist inclinations or urges that were left inside him. Laborers and workers were ordered to extend past their solid cutoff points and any endeavor to wander out of the line was repelled heartlessly. Death camps which were at first set up to rebuff the recent traditionalists and landowners for their past overabundances, started to expand in size taking care of upon honest residents and Communist nonconformists also. The party fanned out into every one of the branches of legislative organization and the Soviet Union was gradually starting to look like a 'Police State' lastingly watchful and hopelessly jumpy with regards to its security and existence.

The Soviet Union subsequent to enduring its first danger to existence with a considerable measure of progress was to awaken to another without further ado. Vladimir Lenin, the unequaled progressive who joined the entire of in reverse Russia under one flag, kicked the bucket rashly in 1922 at the time of 54.

MAN OF STEEL

CHAPTER II

Twin Towers

he demise of the originator patriarch Vladimir Lenin, shocked the Soviet individuals despite the fact that it was very notable that he was incapacitated for a really long time. Lenin's New Economic Policy presented in 1921 a couple of months before his demise, had to an entirely significant degree pacified the disappointed individuals who had been denied of their essential basic liberties. The NEP, as it was called, energized private responsibility for and market valuing of their grain which thusly gave the ranchers solid drive to utilize new techniques for cultivating and increment creation. The expanded food creation alleviated food deficiencies and starvations which by implication killed the insubordinate impulses of the majority. Individuals were gradually becoming accustomed to one more type of dictator initiative however they still truly accepted that better fates lay coming up for them.

The demise of Lenin, for sure had made an extraordinary vacuum at the most significant level of the Soviet administration and onlookers abroad were quickly drafting their

celebratory eulogies for the brief upheaval. Lenin during his most recent couple of years had favored Josef Stalin, one of his nearby partners during the progressive years, to succeed him, yet before long started to falter from his situation for quite some time. Stalin was known to be savage and conspiring during his stretch with the public authority and hosted distanced a great deal of gathering originators with his narrow minded demeanor. Leon Trotsky, another long-lasting partner of Lenin was a solid competitor for the situation of Lenin's replacement. Some more names were additionally in conflict before long Lenin's demise which eventually set off an extreme power battle inside the party.

Josef Stalin known for his ability in control and political moving, at last arose effective toward the finish of the battle. Stalin, not at all like his replacements was a ruler who accepted power with an unmistakable vision for Soviet Russia and thus in numerous ways filled the essential need of uniting Communist control over its immense, various scene. Stalin, most importantly, effectively tackled the issue of various ethnicities competing against each other for matchless quality by carrying out by and by with significant achievement, Lenin's comprehensive hypothesis of patriotism. Numerous dialects having a place with different networks were given inclination in school educational plan also in regulatory issues. The viability of this arrangement in establishing the different ethnicities into the expansive Communist alliance can't be underestimated.

'War Communism' presented by Lenin just on a crisis premise, was systematized under Stalin and truth be told, further strengthened all around the Union. This convention with a couple of additional contributions from Stalin came to be known as 'communism Leninism'. Marx who imagined 'aggregate type of property' for the Communist future accepted uniquely in a transformative type of cultural turn of events, which implied society letting itself from the chains free from feudalism, moving gradually into private enterprise and associatively into a condition of impractical disparity which thusly would prepare for State Socialism at last coming full circle in what is known as Stateless Communism. Lenin as well, during his time as a progressive, had dissected the Russian primitive conditions and hypothetically excused the opportunities for a Communist Revolution in the country. Indeed, even Marx years and years before Lenin, expected a Communist Revolution sooner rather than later, just in an exceptionally industrialized nation like Germany or Britain and not positively in a regressive, immature and medieval Russia. However, what occurred in Russia in 1917 was

an inquisitive blend of elements that were drained to the limit by a clever Marxist legislator in Lenin, because of which the Communists came to control all over Eastern Europe.

Unite or be killed:

Stalin was too eager to even consider permitting Russia to go through its Marxist 'developmental' stages and consequently chose to compel Communism down the throats of the reluctant people. Lands that were appropriated by Lenin to workers during the beginning of the Soviet government, were announced to be surrendered to the State alongside other private property. Ranchers were absolutely reluctant to allow the State to assume control over their territories and assets because of which there was a spike in the quantity of uprisings and unrests by late 1930s. These unsettling influences were savagely smothered by Stalin's incredible hardware and inhumane imprisonments in Siberia were permitted to prosper towards phenomenal sizes. Secret police who came to be known as KGB later, wandered all around the nation and any indications of dispute or dissent were rashly distinguished and reasonably killed. One more gathering supported by Stalin was the Communist Youth League which was loaded with youthful 'revolutionaries' whose principle obligation was helping the police in removing question. Dread spread all around the nation and individuals quit talking about legislative issues openly puts dreading reprisal.

Anyway the main result of collectivisation was a lofty fall in horticultural result and uncontrolled starvation and deficiencies all around the Union. Ranchers were not able to work for concessions and were angry with the State for redirecting an enormous piece of the agrarian result towards urban areas and modern towns. Stalin right from the start was exceptionally restless to assemble Russia's picture for the West, as a quickly industrializing nation all set to overwhelm its entrepreneur rivals. Despite the fact that Stalin prevailed with regards to industrializing Russia through steel and combat hardware ventures, the human and monetary expense caused was huge and to a great extent avoidable. Ukraine lost just about 3 million individuals in 1933 to man-made starvations and neediness. Stalin then again was utilizing all that he can to support his picture through State purposeful publicity instruments like the radio and the press. Russia was depicted to its kin and outside as a country on the cusp of a significant Communist change, which enraptured assessment in the downturn hit entrepreneur countries.

More with regards to Russia's instrumental job in a roundabout way impacting the legislative issues of different nations will be found in the forthcoming chapters.

Fascism and Russia:

Just like what Communist Russia was meaning for the downturn hit Capitalist West, the ascent of Hitler in Germany sent shivers all through the world. Communist history specialists appropriately called 'Totalitarianism' the most exceptional phase of Laissez Faire Capitalism where all relics of average progressivism and vote based system are blown to bits. Hitler firmly enraptured sentiments all around the world prompting extremist developments in Spain, Poland, Japan and so on One party rule in Europe was completely hostile to Semitic and Jews all around the world were seen with doubt and dread. Blacks in the US were comparably abused particularly when the financial downturn was at its peak.

People all around the downturn hit nations began searching for monetary options both in Germany and Russia. Individuals quit trusting in parliamentary vote based system and sat tight for the development of solid, charming pioneers and people who could settle on choices all alone. This was additionally when Communist Parties in Western nations started to assemble gigantic mass help and thusly compromised the discretionary authority of the until now predominant anti-extremist powers. These Communist coalitions were essential for a Communist International drove by the Russian Communist Party (Lenin's group of the RSDLP turned into the Russian Communist Party in 1918) and straightforwardly answered to Josef Stalin in different occasional meetings. The political lines to be taken on in their separate nations were directed by Stalin and his clique, and any deviation by the homegrown authority was managed harshly. Subsequently, these gatherings sang paeans to Communist Russia and its modern accomplishments and guaranteed individuals with an extreme passed on wing option in contrast to all their financial problems.

ussia, thusly drove the counter Fascist coalition while the Soviet press denounced Hitler and his strategies keeping individuals mindful of the always present danger of despotism. At the point when liberal popularity based forerunners in different nations like Britain, US and France were attempting to mollify Hitler and moderate his aspirations, Stalin's Russia continued to show a virtual center finger to the Fascist coalition. Stalin was persistently sending sensors toward the Western nations to shape an authority United Front against Hitler however was censured over and over. Intelligent people all around the world were intrigued with the hypothetical sufficiency of Marxist investigation of Fascism and were induced to join recently mushrooming Fascist Resistance developments in their separate nations. In numerous ways, the way that Communists and left wing extremists initiated the International Resistance developments against despotism is past doubt.

A Spanish debacle:

In 1936, an expansive left wing alliance government headed by the Spanish Communists won the races in Spain. Dreading socialist extension to other adjoining regions, Hitler helped the Spanish General Francisco Franco to arrange a tactical overthrow against the justly chosen government. The tactical upset was effective and an extremist government under Franco was going to be introduced. This set off fights all over Spain and the remainder of the world which before long changed into what was known as the Spanish Civil War of 1936. The Spanish Communist faction, the Trotskyist party (POUM) alongside other left wing parties toward one side (known as Republicans) upheld by great many regular folks from across the world and the Spanish Nationalist Army upheld by Hitler and Mussolini at the opposite end (Nationalists) went into a direct outfitted clash. Stalin felt constrained to help the Spanish Communist reason and sent a segment of his Red Army to battle the fundamentalist Nationalist Army.

Soon the 'Elder sibling' disposition of the Soviet Union went to the front as the Red Army requested the remainder of the Republican soldiers to subordinate to them for vital purposes. The Spanish Republicans submitted hesitantly however the Russian Red Army submitted various key mistakes bringing about various Republican passings. Additionally the Red Army revealing straightforwardly to Stalin was consistently dubious of POUM unit for their Trotskyist leanings. Before long the pressures started to surface and the Republican camp was lease with virtual infighting.

This made the mathematically mediocre Nationalist camp more remarkable than its Republican rival and before the finish of 1939, General Franco and his soldiers figured out how to overcome the Republicans. Franco quickly requested the cleansing of thousands of Republican supporters in Spain, and the promontory stayed fundamentalist till his passing in 1975.

Aftermath of the Spanish Civil war:

The triumph of the Republicans in the Spanish parliamentary decisions in 1936 had given desires to a great many individuals across Europe who feared the looming Fascist risk. Hitler needed to annexe the entire of Europe and subsequently upheld General Franco's soldiers, to join Spain into his Fascist coalition. The Republican side drove by Communists produced extraordinary compassion from all regions of the planet including India which gave clinical and monetary guide under the oversight of Jawaharlal Nehru. Regular people from England, France and some socialist nations joined the Republican cause

and forfeited their lives enthusiastically. All the more critically, Stalin's Russia helped in preparing support for Spain from everywhere the world, because of which the USSR held onto the moral higher ground for some time. The tactical help from USSR was enormous and during the beginning of the conflict, intelligent people started to take an exceptionally thoughtful perspective on Stalin.

Petty inside philosophical conflicts, tyrannical demeanor of Soviet warriors towards their Spanish friends, Stalin's aloofness towards giving guide to Spain in the critical periods of the conflict were a portion of the variables that prompted the loss of the Republican side. The Spanish fiasco wound up seriously harming the confidence of the International (Anti-Fascist) Resistance development which before long were to confront one more blow as the Ribbentrop-Molotov settlement of 1939.

CHAPTER III

Theoretical Detour

Before we get further into the story, a fast jump into what basically is implied by Capitalism, Marxism and Fascism will assist us with understanding the philosophical inclinations that drove the fierce occasions of the Second World War (1939-1945).

Capitalism - Origins:

The time of 'Illumination' in Europe is extensively accepted to start from the French upset of 1779. The French insurgency denoted the loss of the medieval classes and the respectability because of the commercial and the common laborers. Accordingly, the commercial classes (who overwhelmed worldwide exchange) being the richer among the two, normally expected political and financial authority over that of the other, all through Europe (the French Revolution set off comparable emergencies in the remainder of European nations and guaranteed the disappointment of ministry honorability primitive aggregate for the trade classes).

The trade classes before long grew up to become Industrial entrepreneurs with the approach of the Great Industrial Revolution of the last part of the 1700s. Motorized creation of products broke until now existing social bonds and made fresher types of relationship among the majority. Primitive agribusiness quickly gave way to current businesses and tremendous masses of workers needed to adjust to the changing requirements of the recently made 'market'. Ranchers, craftsmans, clerics and such lost their customary servitude to their separate occupations to solidify into one homogenous entire called as the 'Modern Proletariat'. In years and years, this rebuilding of cultural and financial relations started to

effectsly affect the mind of the normal European.

The new-conceived European laborer currently felt one with a great deal of other modern specialists like him and his limited, crude personalities were quickly vanishing. He before long understood that he was more exhausted than previously and the advantages of his diligent effort, he discovered a lot to his caution, were being shared more inconsistent than previously. Likewise his insight into conventional artworks like earthenware, weaving, coloring, and so forth were at this point not pertinent, as machines and bores delivered more merchandise with substantially less exertion and time. In enormous processing plants where the division of work was at the most elevated, all his work was limited to extra and administrative obligations. This before long prompted a horrible estrangement among himself and his result since he had just an extremely insignificant job in delivering it. Outrageous division of work prompted enormous work deskilling while an exceptionally slanted circulation of made abundance began creating outrageous pay imbalances. The political results of these abrupt and unexpected changes were additionally similarly critical. Communist thoughts spread all over Europe which focused on the requirement for coordination of the regular workers rising above public and racial hindrances. Worker's organizations were manufactured dependent on the newly discovered 'ordinary solidarity' whose potential for aggregate haggling filled in as a stabilizer to the decision/taking advantage of classes. In numerous ways by late 1800s, Britain, France, Germany and other industrialized European countries saw the solidification of various races, clans and networks of individuals into two wide surmised classes-the entrepreneur and the low class (common laborers). This period of financial development was, in Marxist terms, called the Capitalist phase.

What was good in Capitalism?

The upgrades accomplished in intercontinental marine, the creation of the steam motor combined with quick spread of 'Illumination' values like secularism, opportunity of articulation, grown-up establishment, logical viewpoint and human correspondence freed European masses from their extremely old medieval chains and drove them into the Age of Industrial Capitalism. Without precedent for mankind's set of experiences, a huge number of individuals from various topographical areas and different foundations began working under one rooftop for a solitary entrepreneur. Ware creation during the past period was negligible, as in a weaver in the town of Leicester, on the vast majority of events, made fabric for a couple of craftsman miles from his home. The interest henceforth, was for the most part nearby and creation, thusly was just restricted though under Capitalism, request was less neighborhood than in any case and

accordingly, creation was unavoidably enormous scope. To meet both interior and outer interest for modern items, horticulture was informally debilitate and a worker evacuated from a town like Yorkshire had to hobnob with one more laborer from Manchester while holding up in the long, serpentine line to get his every day wage from his new processing plant boss. Races, societies, dialects and religions broke down rapidly into the mixture of metropolitan civilisation which denoted the start of another part during the time spent social evolution.

The trading of various thoughts alongside the developing prominence of way breaking logical hypotheses (Darwin's hypothesis of normal determination assumed a colossal part) constrained average people to return to their adherences to customary strict conviction frameworks. The capacity of science to investigate, clarify and anticipate normal peculiarities before long started to break the authority of nearby pastors. Disobedience of ministers and clerics by the everyday citizens before long implied insubordination of respectability and serfdom. In the vast majority of the nations, lands were possessed by Churches and aristocrats whose techniques for double-dealing of the working class were vigorously subject to painstakingly safeguarded offbeat convictions. Diocese supervisors and godmen made nearby laws without a similarity to vote based system, in close nexus with the aristocrats and the illustrious executives. The change to modern Capitalism, thusly implied the overwhelming and minimization of totally informal and outdated relations of creation which left the disappointed decision classes sticking around for their opportunity for revenge.

hat makes Capitalism dig its own grave?

"What the bourgeoisie, along these lines, produces, most importantly, is its own undertakers. Its fall and the triumph of the working class are similarly inevitable"

This was Karl Marx in the last part of the 1800s when Industrial Europe was awakening to the unexpected, yet sensational impacts of the new entrepreneur relations of production.

Let us first gander at why Capitalism is frequently compared with 'double-dealing' by Marxist journalists. Free enterprise, as per Marx makes due on the main state of 'collection of excess worth'. Excess worth here alludes to the measure of work that a laborer offers to the industrialist, more than whatever he is paid for*. Under Capitalism, on each and every day, a laborer is compelled to sell his work at a cost that approaches just the expense of recharging his laboring potential for one more day of work. In any case, the ware he delivers and hands over to the industrialist has a 'market' esteem which is twice than what he is being paid**. This extraction of excess work power

out of the laborer assists the industrialist with getting a lopsidedly bigger portion of made riches. Consequently this arrangement of creation relations breeds financial imbalance prompting a steadily enlarging gorge between the rich and the poor.

With the headway in innovation, entrepreneurs think that it is more straightforward to supplant work with hardware and this thus makes an extremely durable modern hold multitude of jobless individuals. The more the entrepreneur amasses, the more his propensity to automate creation and the more motorized an industry gets, more number of individuals wind up scrambling for a quickly contracting number of occupations. Consequently the presence of a modern save armed force assists the entrepreneur with keeping compensation low and concentrate more labour.

During the start of the industrialist cycle when the stock is reasonably fulfilled by proportionate need, the economy is perfectly healthy as the homegrown utilization is higher and the developing interest for merchandise, thusly makes an ever increasing number of occupations (Boom). More positions implies more cash on account of the laborers to spend and consequently the cycle proceeds productively. Contest among organizations will in general decrease market costs and an attending overproduction of products triggers collapse and a further descending twisting of costs. To make up at the falling costs which implies a lower pace of benefit, the entrepreneur resorts to supplanting work with hardware. However, soon at a specific crossroads, the impracticality of the cycle rises to the top when all the contending business people resort to motorization of creation setting off an influx of specialist conservation. At the point when more laborers wind up out of occupations, their utilization lessens which thusly diminishes homegrown interest. Lesser interest can be met with lesser work and lesser apparatus and this tosses one more balance of laborers of the labor force. This cycle fabricates and constructs and all we have toward the end is a horrible period of stagnation and pervasive destitution (Bust).

During these periods of bust, the laborers wind up adrift and search for political answers for their monetary issues. The primitive time didn't deliver a lot of merchandise and subsequently scarcely offered any degree for enormous one-sided gathering by one specific class. The feudalist framework commanded a specific portion of the farming produce to be given over by the turner to the landowner and permitted him to save the rest for himself. Craftsmans and specialists worked in shared arrangements called organizations which included networks of individuals dealing with both creation and advertising themselves. The made worth, thus was being dispersed more

or less similarly among themselves and the extension for abuse was very negligible. In particular, the primitive time saw exceptionally less joblessness despite the fact that neediness was generally prevalent.

ut without precedent for history under private enterprise, the human culture observed itself to be enormously inconsistent as well as, interestingly, unquestionably pregnant with a new and an extreme thought cultivated by the best upsides of European Enlightenment and fed by the savage abundances of entrepreneur double-dealing, whose time for rise, it was broadly accepted, had luckily come.

Why Marxism?

Falling wages and rising joblessness, necessary extra time for laborers, work deskilling and specialist 'distance', inescapable destitution and developing starvation, consistently expanding pay imbalances, all of which together would in general drive the normal European to outrageous distress. He was frightfully befuddled concerning why he was unable to purchase sufficient bread in any event, when there was an excess on the lookout. He was unable to comprehend the reason why out of nowhere the information on his acquired occupation was considered totally futile. He was unable to see how marbled palatial houses and extravagance cafés sprang alongside cesspools spotted with frightful shacks and residue covered cottages. He was unable to comprehend the reason why a jobless grown-up was regarded under a youngster worker inside a family. He was unable to comprehend the reason why an ever increasing number of individuals were starting to turn to any means whatsoever, to separate an additional a penny from the other.

The distributing of Das Kapital in 1867 by Karl Marx took a drawn-out period of time to trigger torrents that it was intended to, in political and scholarly circles. Marx composed one more magnum opus which passed by the name 'The Communist Manifesto' as a team with his companion Friedrich Engels. These original books alongside a couple of more came to shape the hypothetical premise of Marxian Socialism.

Marx was the primary famous scholarly in Europe to dissect, contextualize and anticipate the future advancement of Industrial Capitalism consequently responding to practically every one of the inquiries of the confounded normal European. The Communist Manifesto imagined an Utopian culture of things to come that would exist without an administration where individuals did occupations that they were normally great at and adequately made to fulfill their day by day essential requirements. Individuals imparted all work to one another in little agglomerations called Communes where social, racial and monetary orders had no business to exist. The absence of a

government implied total shortfall of a police power since it was accepted that a Communist society would have no double-dealing and thus no degree for wrongdoing. Individuals were to be passed judgment on dependent on what they really prepared to do rather than by the measure of monetary worth they made. As such, Communism required the total devastation of customarily severe, social, racial and financial constructions and welcomed each specialist, laborer and skilled worker in each nation to break up himself in the extraordinary global ordinary ocean.

As you might see, Communist thoughts had a lot of motivations to speak to enormous masses of individuals across nations and mainlands coaxing every one of them to participate in the progressive battle against the taking advantage of propertied classes. Communism, at the end of the day required a logical, objective and populist society which spelt nothing under a considerable danger to the presence of all presently domineering classes that have been flourishing up until recently simply dependent on exploitation.

hy Fascism?

To precisely characterize the philosophical forms of autocracy is a totally pointless undertaking since dictatorship is everything except philosophical. Extremism can reasonably be decreased to a coherent estimate of many-shaded at this point consistently hasty calls for self-preservation by all the current or quickly lessening authoritative classes because of the certain danger from the displeased proletariat.

Any country viable, it is to be noted, doesn't move flawlessly from one type of creation relations into one more overall, in one single stroke. Primitive or semi medieval structures may coincide for some time with cutting edge industrialist structures until the last option burns-through the previous totally. Thus, these medieval classes do keep on existing, applying their impact on public legislative issues too regardless of whether their essence is simple. In different nations, these primitive classes structure the foundation of conservative fundamentalist developments helping individuals to remember their pre-industrialist characters like race, religion and networks. Their impact on popular assessment is never to be disparaged on the grounds that character legislative issues proves to be useful in any event, for their industrialist partners to break the solidarity of the rising proletariat.

When the majority are confounded with respect to why they stay poor and denied of chances in any event, when public abundance overall is expanding, just Marxism reacts to them precisely by pointing fingers at the taking advantage of propertied classes. Exclusively to counter this test, Fascism lingers up to quickly redirect the consideration of the majority from the propertied classes

towards the actual majority, accusing everything on a little racial or strict or a public minority with the end goal of breaking their recently discovered lowly solidarity. This can be seen better assuming we relate this peculiarity to that happening in India under the current Hindu Nationalist system where the foundation continues to fault Muslims and Pakistanis at whatever point awkward inquiries in regards to economy are raised.

Fascism, as well as assaulting Marxism doesn't avoid focusing on the upsides of 'Illumination' too secularism, radicalism, logical standpoint, majority rule government and free discourse, and so on exclusively on the grounds that these standards were instrumental in the development of the Marxist hypothesis. To put it plainly, Fascism is against whatever is considered moderate, and subsequently regularly alluded in like manner speech as completely 'traditionalist' in nature.

Now that we are adequately side by side of the philosophical premise of mid twentieth century European emergency, we can easily get back to our story.

conomic Depression of 1929 and rise of Fascism:

By the finish of the 1920s, the modern United States and Western Europe had depleted the 'blast' period of their entrepreneur cycle and were quick lessening into the unavoidable period of 'bust'. 1929 was the year when an extraordinary Stock Market decline happened in the US which set off a falling financial breakdown in all nations industrially connected to the monetary superpower. Italy, France, Germany, Britain and other exchanging accomplices of US were the most exceedingly terrible hit with a great many laborers losing positions regular consequently setting off an emergency in practically all areas of their public economies.

The Russian Revolution which had introduced a Communist Government in charge of the biggest country on the planet, had been rousing Communist developments in practically all areas of the planet since the time 1917. Since the finish of the First World War, Germany was giving all indications of appropriately following the Russian model when the electing impact of the German Communist Party was developing complex. In equal, uncommon conditions, for example, the burden of the embarrassing Versailles settlement on Germany by the wide range of various Western powers toward the finish of the WW1 and the destroying of the Second Reich simultaneously to clear way for popular government, likewise had given fundamental and adequate justification for the restoration of German nationalism.

The collaboration of Communist and the antagonist Nationalist impacts on the mind of the normal German delivered wonderful cultural outcomes. The financial downturn whose effects were show in the mid 1930s

crushed all open trust in the parliamentary arrangement of vote based system and drove Germans to track down arrangements in tyrant models. Vital bumbles on numerous occasions by the German Communist faction alongside the hesitance of the middle passed on Social Democrats to adequately analyze the degree of the Fascist disease prompted the electing triumph of Adolf Hitler's National Socialist Party (Nazi) in 1933. The Nazi party developed on inborn, yet simple enemy of semitism of the Germans and enhanced it lopsidedly to suit its political closures. The financial difficulties of the nation were accused on both the Jews and the Western Powers and Hitler called for segregation of the neighborhood Jews to guarantee Aryan racial immaculateness. German Fascism roused comparative developments in Poland, Austria and surprisingly in the United States.

Keep your friends close, enemies closer:

Hitler expected power in 1933 and before long passed a progression of acts that were pointed toward subverting popularity based organizations. The Communist faction was restricted and an extraordinary cleanse of Communist and worker's organization chiefs followed. Jews were handpicked from each niche and corner of the nation's roads and compelled to work in ghettos (inhumane imprisonments). Hitler annulled the post of the President with the passing of Hindenburg and announced himself, the sole Chancellor of Germany. He called his new Government 'the Third Reich', a reference to Germany's apparently sublime a long time under government.

The ascent of Hitler frightened socialists all around the world and his partnership with Italian Fascist tyrant Benito Mussolini raised a great deal of eyebrows in the Western Capitalist camp too. Hitler continued to menace his more modest sovereign neighbors with Nazi military may and continued to sign a series of deals permitting German venture into the West. A large portion of these settlements were honored by the hesitance of French, British and American Governments to stand up to Hitler since these nations were not generally before the finish of the 1930s prepared to wander into another conflict. Russia's Stalin kept on calling for vital partnerships with the Western Powers to counter the danger of Hitler and kept his promulgation hardware staying at work longer than required to keep individuals all around the world ever careful to the rising danger of Fascism. Socialist coalitions all around the world were requested by Stalin to start to lead the pack in countering nearby extremist developments. At the point when none of the Western Powers reacted emphatically to his calls, Stalin had to fight for himself at the end.

Hitler before the finish of 1938 had figured out how to re-arm Germany to its pre-1914 strength. A great many imprints were spent on arms and ammo fabricating while the size of the German military developed manifold

during the Nazi years. Hitler was presently setting his sights far higher. He needed to bring the entire of Europe under his influence however was similarly careful about the danger presented by his Communist neighbor. He wasn't prepared by then of time to open a conflict at two fronts all the while and thus chose to save Russia for the future.

o he required a peace concurrence with Russia to which a frantic Stalin submitted promptly, finishing in the Molotov-Ribbentrop settlement endorsed on August 23, 1939 at Moscow. The agreement perceived common power and commanded non-impedance into one another's expansionist points. Also, Germany and Russia perceived common 'ranges of prominence' in Europe later on occasion of a potential revamp of regions having a place with Poland and the Baltic nations. Hitler's hand was immensely reinforced by this noteworthy settlement with Stalin which impelled him to assault Poland the exceptionally one week from now on September 1, 1939, that remarkable date frequently viewed as the date of the start of the Second World War.

Stalin, then again knew very well that the main substantial benefit that the agreement had given him was just a between time breathing space that could empower him to anticipate the frightful unavoidable - that last go head to head against the considerable Germany, which was relied upon to happen sooner than later, regardless of whether Hitler was ending up bizarrely affable to him, for the time being.

*a undeniably challenging endeavor has been made by me to work on Marxist hypothesis of excess worth however much as could reasonably be expected. I thusly recognize the conceivable mistake of my statement regarding what Marx had really said.

**the costs and qualities were determined by Marx in Capital Volume 1 dependent on speculative market conditions.

CHAPTER IV

lood, Blood Everywhere

Josef Stalin, when he took on the position in 1922 was at first viewed as a commendable replacement to the tradition of the organizer chief Vladimir Lenin by the majority. Stalin endeavored to expand on that picture and attempted to set up a faction of character wherever in and around Russia. State media were requested to sing 'paeans' to Stalin and his persona while it was likewise a fact that the majority purchased that 'picture' faithfully. Socialist factions of different nations, partnered to the Communist International were additionally compelled to bow

before Stalin's matchless quality and nonconformists assuming any, were removed regardless of whether their earnestness to the development was past doubt.

ut Stalin, actually like some other tyrant had a lot of frailties. Hosting gone through the idiocies of intra-get-together power battles himself, Stalin was awkward at the possibility of experiencing political controllers (like him) and other well known progressives who may, at a startling place of time, given the absence of legitimate intra party majority rules system, have a special interest in initiative. Likewise, Stalin's fixation on quick outcomes as for economy which may assist with approving his political prevalence started over have absolutely unexpected and nauseating consequences.

When Stalin requested constrained collectivisation of farming, laborers who got land during Lenin's NEP begun revolting. Uprisings spread all through Russia which just wound up inspiring much additional harsh measures from the State. Before long, a large number of ranchers were shipped off Siberian inhumane imprisonments where they were passed on to work the entire day and stick to no end. Inside two or three years, the results of constrained collectivisation were felt all around the country with thousands biting the dust from food deficiencies and cruel working conditions.

The decision Communist Party which actually had a solid number of sacrificial and committed author individuals in its positions, was starting to break separated. Stalin's approaches came up for conversation during party gatherings and searing allegations were heaved facing him by party groups drove by Leon Trotsky. Nikolai Bukharin, one more famous originator part now in Stalin's camp was soon to join the resistance. With an enormous number of well known pioneers energizing against Stalin, what he did close to hold power, was essentially unmatched in its ruthlessness and scale, by some other occasion in mankind's set of experiences so far.

Gliding over all:

1933 was the year when Stalin's assistant Sergei Kirov was bafflingly killed. This was trailed by a progression of executions of all well known pioneers who wouldn't fall in line of Stalin. Large number of party pioneers, laborers and scholarly people who had surrendered all their own aspirations for seeing the making of Communist Russia during their lifetime were formally proclaimed 'counter-progressives' and consequently executed right away. Before long the cleanse stretched out into different spaces too - researchers, craftsmen, educators, military faculty, association pioneers, officials, engineers who were associated with hostile to Stalinism were found and removed. Indeed, even individuals who had been recently connected with Trotsky however had later exchanged camps were not prohibited. A masterpiece which had no reference to the 'brilliance of the Revolution', a legitimate logical contention that contradicted the public authority's arrangement, an article in the paper that seemed as though appreciating the West were sufficient and adequate confirmations as to warrant preliminary and abuse. The majority of the Communist chiefs were exposed to physical and mental torment and had to sign 'intentional' admissions of having enjoyed 'demonstrations of injustice and damage'. Eric Hobsbawm, a left wing British student of history in one of his expositions specifies that because of both man-made starvation and Stalin's cleanses, the yearly development pace of the whole Soviet Population itself fell radically during the 1930s and required a few years to rebound.

Leon Trotsky who figured out how to get away from Soviet Russia, following various long stretches of dynamic political life in the West was killed in Mexico in 1940. Before the finish of 1938, the Communist Party had been cleaned off of Stalin's doubters and even of those rare sorts of people who had some autonomous line of thinking. Stalin carried some more changes to the Soviet constitution to make him the most remarkable innovator in the entire of the Union. Vesting practically all dynamic powers into the situation of the General Secretary of the Party would have telling outcomes in the future including that of the defeat of the Soviet Union itself.

Stalin joins Hitler's party:

Hitler assaulted Poland on September 1, 1939 which welcomed both England and France into the World War. Poland fell inside half a month and the Soviet Union was welcome to share the crown jewels. Baltic nations like Latvia, Estonia and Lithuania were additionally before long attached by Soviet powers supported by the Nazi soldiers. Before long the Soviet Union and the Nazis consented to a reciprocal exchange arrangement which guaranteed shared trade of food, buyer durables and military gear throughout the war.

he Russo-Nazi joint activity in Europe was an awful shame for Communist factions world over which had been up until now, ardent and resolute in their resistance to Fascism. Be that as it may, the gatherings were not prepared to estrange Soviet assistance for their nearby exercises and consequently chose to toe Stalin's line obediently. An enormous number of persuasive financial specialists and scholarly people all over Europe quit the Communist coalition during this time as more monstrosities were going to follow. The KGB authorities gave a great deal of German socialists who were up until recently given political shelter in the USSR to the German State Police in adherence to specific mystery rules in the Ribbentrop-Molotov pact.

By 1940, Germany and USSR had developed so near one another that the previous welcomed the last option to join the Axis Powers and battle the West as a solitary durable coalition. In any case, the Soviet Union was, in equal out of control over its past domains (of the Tsarist period) adding Finland and ravaging Romania all of which somewhat upset Hitler. Additionally there were a few conflicts over boundary in the caught domains between the Nazi and Red Army bosses which, but were commonly consented to be settled for the time being.

The beginning of the end of Adolf Hitler:

Hitler right from his days as a road government official held onto resentment towards Communists and the Slavs. In his life account Mein Kampf, he had expounded on his fantasies about bringing the entire of Russia under Aryan guideline. When he expected power, his first objective was the Communists followed by the Jews and other 'substandard' races like the Slavs. Regardless of whether Hitler busied himself with endeavors to pay Britain and France in similar coin for their conniving endeavors in embarrassing Germany through the Versailles, Soviet Russia was consistently at the rear of his mind.

But nothing encouraged him to assault Russia in 1941 itself as much as his gigantic military triumphs over Poland, Denmark, Belgium, Norway and Luxembourg. In particular, Hitler was thrilled when Nazi soldiers alongside those of Italy, vanquished France inside only 46 days of battle. By December 1940, just inside short of what one and half long periods of the beginning of the Great War, Germany had figured out how to bring the greater part of Western Europe under its thumb.

Hitler's notoriety took off all over Nazi Germany and he was viewed as the genuine replacement to the superb tradition of the recent Reich Empire. Till 1940, Hitler had resisted a ton of counsel given by his tactical commanders and simple, nonstop triumphs did an extraordinary arrangement to support his certainty. His carelessness was soon in plain view in the start of 1941 when he was poring over Germany's arrangements to assault the Soviet Union. Hitler was right in expecting that Stalin had cleansed a larger part of his top military staff during the 1930s itself and henceforth needed to depend on unpracticed authorities in case of a conflict. Hitler additionally took a gander at the extremely sluggish advancement made by the Red Army against the as far as anyone knows powerless Finns throughout the Winter War of 1939-40 and felt that he could securely depend on the awkwardness of the Soviet military machine in his arrangements to propel his assault on the Soviet Union, essentially by a year.

Hitler likewise accepted that the Russian residents were awfully mistreated by

Stalin and his malleable administration and subsequently a German attack would perhaps be invited by them as a method towards their freedom. He should have commented to his associates, 'We will simply kick the entryway of the house and I am certain the entire construction will come down!'

Stalin then again, disregarded alerts radiating from Britain and his own mysterious assistance about an approaching Nazi intrusion in mid-1941 and firmly accepted that Hitler would not be prepared to open a conflict on two fronts at the same time. Hitler in the interim was preparing his soldiers for a conflict against Russia which he needed to be exceptionally boorish in its savagery, disregarding all codes of fighting. Actually like how the Nazis had killed in excess of 1,000,000 Poles when they involved Poland, the Wehrmacht (Unified military of Germany) were told to be similarly severe on Russian regular folks and to plunder all their material belongings to help further Nazi advance.

Hitler instituted another name for his mission against Russia, disregarding critical admonitions by his commanders on environment and coordinations and dispatched Operation Barbarossa on June 22, 1941.

HAPTER V

he Wall

nspite of constrained collectivisation of agribusiness and resulting mass discontent over Stalin's arrangements, the over accentuation on industrialisation was starting to create impressive financial development in the USSR. At the point when the Industrial West was reeling under the eventual outcomes of financial downturn, the USSR inspite of formally swelled figures, was viewed as a developing economy by different business analysts. Financial preparation by the Center which was contradictory to the industrialist method of creation was presently seen well by the entrepreneur nations impacted by the Depression. Soviet Industrial result was immensely reliant upon the tactical necessities of Russia directed by Stalin's noteworthy premonition. However there were bombed modern investigations to a great extent, the Soviet Economy figured out how to repay by expanding the functioning hours of the modern workers substantially.

The USSR before the finish of 1930s, had a superior modern economy, dramatically more prominent military strength both as far as men and ammo, a more focused administration and a more noteworthy mass of controlled party framework than it had during the past turbulent decade. These were perspectives that Hitler may have neglected to face during the drafting of the plans for

Operation Barbarossa.

Since the time the finish of the Ribbentrop-Molotov settlement in 1939, the USSR media thought that it is practical to restrain against Fascist promulgation all together not to incite Hitler. Indeed, even by mid 1941, when indications of Nazi antagonism were starting to surface, Stalin couldn't force himself to consider the potential outcomes of a Nazi intrusion that very year, except if a plain incitement was produced using their end. Anyway this was actually what Hitler had gravely required - an unexpected assault that would daze Stalin into wretched submission.

First Blood:

Hitler overpowered by triumphs over Western Europe was light when Britain began giving indications of breaking under tenacious air assaults by the German Luftwaffe. Also Operation Barbarossa, he assumed would end inside two or three months with Stalin giving up to the absolutely unanticipated Nazi mobilization.

The activity which started in June 1941 was multi-pronged with fronts being opened on all sides of the world's biggest country with an inflexible expectation to obliterate the Russians. Soviet obstruction was clearly frail and they failed to keep a grip on Northern Finland, Ukraine, Belarus by September 1941. Hitler was glad to have taken the city of Smolensk which had a direct 400 km street to Moscow and the Nazi press was euphoric to illuminate the German masses that they were only half a month from a noteworthy triumph over Russia.

But Nazi troopers, in spite of their assumptions acknowledged soon that the Russian regular folks were not prepared to double-cross their nation with such ease. Truth be told, to their shock, the Nazis could see countless regular citizens effectively enrolling in the Red Army with extraordinary enthusiasm particularly when Leningrad went under attack. The laborers prior to escaping their towns ensured that their harvests were singed, dairy cattle killed and assets obliterated to deny the trespassers of essential supplies. Hitler's transition to dispatch Barbarossa sooner than arranged was vigorously subject to the chance of capture of Russian assets for Nazi military purposes yet the Scorched Earth strategy of the Russians was totally startling. Their transition to take Ukraine's capital Kiev which was brimming with oil assets negatively affected their military strength despite the fact that they prevailed in their central goal eventually.

By October 1941, Hitler was getting reports of triumphs on all fronts in USSR despite the fact that protests of supply deficiencies were gradually springing up. He currently squeezed his men forward to take Moscow next which, as we shall

see was an awful essential mistake, for it was exactly when winter was setting rapidly all over Western Russia.

Red Heat:

The Nazis were only under 150 km away from Moscow when snow and rains started to harm street lines prompting the capital city. German tanks were not used to such landscape regardless of which by November 1941, the Nazi troopers had the option to unhesitatingly answer to Berlin that they could smell Kremlin only a couple of miles away. Yet, the Russian winter heightened with abrupt snowstorms destroying the landscape. This thusly delivered air assaults absolutely incomprehensible and subsequently German supplies were appallingly hit. The Nazis had no other decision except for to trust that a little while will do any further progress. Stalin then again promptly called the powers on the Siberian front (monitoring the Russo-Japanese lines) and prepared a lot of divisions to safeguard the capital city.

Russian warriors normally had no issues battling in the midst of the tenacious winter and their tanks were better designed to arrange problematic territory. The Soviet fightback close to Moscow was wonderful and the Nazis were effectively removed out of Moscow's area in a drawn out counter hostile. By January 1942, Hitler needed to recognize covertly that the Battle of Moscow was a disaster and that without a modification of procedure, there would be significantly more inversions. In the interim Stalin felt that it was his opportunity to overwhelm Hitler and requested the starting of counter offensives in all German involved domains. He generously expanded expenses for deadly implement and airplane creation. Nazis' resulting endeavors to catch Azerbaijan were additionally seriously frustrated by the Red Army and the increasing winter. Germany likewise ended up seriously ailing in oil to meet its expanding fuel demands.

By mid-1942 itself, the Russians had, attributable to beginning inversions lost near 1,000,000 officers and foundation worth billions. However, Stalin's dynamic authority guaranteed that the confidence of the Red Army and the non military personnel people never dove because of which their troopers faced troublesome conflicts more fearlessly than their German counterparts.

Saviour Stalin:

Two fights that happened in the following two years definitively shifted the direction of the conflict the Battle of Stalingrad (October 1942 - February 1943) and the Battle of Kursk (July to August 1943). Hitler in the wake of confronting inversions at Moscow currently moved his sights onto the modern town called Stalingrad

which filled in as one of the greatest assembling centers in the Soviet Union. The catch of Stalingrad and annihilation of the city, Hitler accepted will stifle the Soviet conflict Economy totally. Nazis likewise needed to hold onto the water courses of Volga River which could undoubtedly be worked with by the catch of Stalingrad. The water courses could assist Germans with overseeing supply lines and furthermore help them in their walk towards oil-rich Baku.

he fight for Stalingrad occurred for north of a half year with Nazis accomplishing key leap forwards at first. Indeed in the initial four months, the Germans caught in excess of the vast majority of the town's region and proceeded to obliterate industrial facilities. The non military personnel populace was not cleared as expected by the Red Army which prompted a ton of setbacks. Anyway the Red Army fighters battled from unusual situations in the city like the sewers, rooms in cleared places of business presenting hardened opposition. Before long the Nazis were floored to see a couple of divisions of the Russian armed force comprising of ladies troopers and surprisingly undeveloped regular people. Towards January 1943, the Sixth Army of the Germans was encircled on all sides by more up to date divisions of the Red Army and all inventory lines from Germany were effectively cut off. Near 200,000 troopers were locked inside the town and they needed to rely entirely upon the provisions from the Luftwaffe. As weeks passed, the meeting Luftwaffe planes were assaulted by those of the Soviet aviation based armed forces and the quantity of usable airplane at the intruder's side was quick waning. By February 1943, Hitler took over as the Chief Commander of the Wehrmacht and he fervently dismissed requests from the Sixth Army to give up at Stalingrad. In the interim, the combat hardware processing plants found east of Urals in Russia were working at full limit and fresher military gear was provided at a fast speed to the Red Army. Before the finish of February, the starving and unsettled Sixth Army chose to give up to the Russians chafing a die-hard Hitler. The skirmish of Stalingrad is viewed as the bloodiest fight in mankind's set of experiences with setbacks on the two sides adding up to millions. Triumph in the clash of Kursk followed that very year for the Russians and by then, at that point, the Germans had for all intents and purposes been driven into the defensive.

Stalin was hailed all around the world for his compelling initiative and the worldwide press had to hail Russians for their magnificent opposition. In the mean time, the tables had turned on in the West with Japan bringing a lethargic United States into the conflict and Hitler needed to supervise military procedure on two fronts none of which were giving uplifting news. Italy's acquiescence to the Allies in 1943 likewise struck a strong hit to the fortunes of Axis

powers. Stalin requested the Red Army to walk into Germany following the freedom of the involved regions. The Wehrmacht was by mid 1945 depleting the German economy while Hitler was quick losing his allies.

Observers in America including top military faculty conceded that Communist Russia practically without any assistance figured out how to stop the unavoidably unsafe Nazi development at an enormous human and financial expense. Near 25 million Russians had been killed during their battle against the Nazis and the Soviet Economy drooped once more into one more crisis.

Adolf Hitler, having been encircled by Allied soldiers on all sides, in May 1945 ended it all at Berlin. The Nazi officers who had slaughtered a great many Jews, POWs in the involved regions were rebuffed at the Nuremberg trials.

Josef Stalin once censured by the world as a wretched savage, had now laid down a good foundation for himself on the planet scene as the Hero who saved the World from the jaws of Fascism. The height of the USSR among the world powers was presently totally evident and this prompted the consideration of the country in the new-conceived United Nations as one of its five Permanent individuals. Yet, the totally sudden rise of USSR as the safeguard of world harmony, sway and correspondence had really enduring and perilous repercussions. From 1945 onwards it would be in Berlin, the world's past wellspring of Fascism that the building to check more current and greater philosophical conflicts of things to come would be developed, as the Wall that partitioned the city into its Western and Eastern halves.

CHAPTER VI

he Swansong

he gigantic triumph accomplished by the USSR in the epochal Second World War had helped support the glory of the Union also that of its ruler. The public mind-set, all around was celebratory and individuals were alleviated that the three-year long conflict which had negatively affected their lives and assets had at last finished. Russia had the option to add-on a ton of regions from different European nations and Stalin foisted Communist Governments in nations like Poland while he was glad to see a couple of like Yugoslavia and Czechoslovakia turning Communist out independently. Yugoslavia had battled on the Allies driven by the courageous Joseph Broz Tito against the Axis Powers and following the conflict the charming Marshal assumed control over the reins of the country with inescapable public help and restricted Soviet assistance. The Baltic nations were likewise brought under Soviet influence

and pretty much every decision Communist Party needed to answer to Stalin on practically all key interior affairs.

Russians, for ages together are regularly accepted to have favored iron fisted leaders over delicate ones and henceforth accommodation to Stalin's absolutism, as per a couple of verifiable records, was treated by the general population as a method of paying respect to their Holy Fatherland. At the point when Russia was maneuvered into 'The Great Patriotic War' in 1942, Stalin's sudden move to restore the traditions of some of Tsarist Russia's recent rulers was met with animating positive energy and extraordinary enthusiasm among the majority. The State promulgation machines conjured the accomplishments of Peter the Great and other unbelievable Tsars and uproarious calls to reestablish the Great Russian Pride were given steadily. Stalin likewise guaranteed that a wide base of public help was accomplished during this season of emergency by speedily loosening up limitations on free discourse and the act of religion. Huge number of detainees were set free from death camps and were relied upon to join the military while Catholic Churches were brought to conform to the State's conflict exertion. Stalin's strategies at the hour of public crisis, obviously proved to be fruitful and it is especially to the credit of the normal Russian fighter that the approaching Fascist plague was destroyed unequivocally from the substance of the Earth (besides in Spain). Individuals, consequently normally expected extremely durable withdrawal of severe measures alongside substantial strides by the State towards advancement of their everyday environments. In any case, what happened later was simply a remarkable opposite.

Tito wags the middle finger:

Marshal Tito, right from the establishment of the Communist Republic in Yugoslavia in 1945 was unwilling to the domineering mentalities of Soviet Russia and was set on taking a free line. He additionally attempted to part the Communist Bloc and structure a different organization to balance over the top Russian impedance. At the point when common conflict broke out in Greece in 1946, Tito much to the vexation of the USSR sent soldiers willingly to help the Grecian Communist camp while Stalin because of a conservative with the Western Powers, had guaranteed them impartiality beating other East European republics to stay quiet. Stalin had likewise established witnesses inside the Yugoslavian Communist Party yet Tito didn't think long and hard about finding and killing them. Tito even before his triumphant military mission against the Axis, had delighted in incredible prevalence among his comrades and consequently had next to no need of Moscow's help to come to power.

Tito's disobedience to Stalin prompted the removal of Yugoslavia from the Communist International (Comintern) in 1948 (until the burst was recuperated in 1955 under an alternate Soviet administration). Anyway Stalin was stressed a lot over Tito starting 'an unfortunate trend' for other satellite nations to follow, that he even made ineffective plans for an attack of Yugoslavia before the finish of the 1940s. Stalin's uncertainty is obvious in one of the letters Tito kept in touch with the previous, which goes as follows: 'Dear Stalin, quit sending your men to kill me. I have caught five of them. Assuming I send one to kill you, there will not be need for a second'.

ussians return to 'normalcy':

The Russian residents then again were to observe something that they had least anticipated. Stalin stunned everybody by requesting downgrade and move of fruitful conflict time military tops of the Red Army to other less amazing positions and continued the 'cleanses' for which he was so infamous for. Sizes of death camps were reestablished nearly to their pre-war levels and social equality were controlled by and by. The majority were admonished to work longer hours and manufacturing plants were set incomprehensible focuses to revive the conflict desolated economy.

Stalin, nonetheless, was gradually subsiding from the middle stage attributable to age related ailments from the last part of the 1940s and different pioneers began assisting him with overseeing day by day undertakings. China in the mean time had prevailed with regards to becoming Communist under the unique initiative of Mao Zedong with solid help from the Soviet Union. The People's Republic of China was set up in 1949 and was relied upon to join the fleeting trend of Soviet's satellites soon. In any case, Moscow was to acknowledge in no time that Mao was not to be taken lightly.

With the Korean War attracting to an impasse in 1953, Josef Stalin, a couple of months before the Korean cease-fire was marked, inhaled his keep going on fifth March at 74 years old. Stalin was covered close by author patriarch Vladimir Lenin at the renowned Lenin's Mausoleum on ninth March within the sight of pioneers from different Soviet satellite states. Numerous nations mourned the dying of the Soviet chief and India's Jawaharlal Nehru broadcasted a solemn vibe in his discourse to the Parliament, loading awards on quite possibly the most confusing leader of history.

In any case an exceptionally incredible figure has died however Marshal Stalin was something considerably more than the top of a State. He was incredible by his own doing way, regardless of whether he involved the workplace or not'.

The third generation:

Josef Stalin, the Georgian progressive turned despot had no question, left the Soviet Union ordinarily more grounded and more powerful in worldwide undertakings than it was before he dominated. It is exclusively to the credit of that man, the child of a helpless shoemaker that the Union made due however long it did. In any case, that doesn't clarify everything about the situation of Stalin in Russia's set of experiences. The ascent of the USSR as a superpower toward the finish of the Second World War, however a marvelous accomplishment given its awful treatment on account of the Western powers in its early stages, was achieved at a humongous expense. A huge number of laborers were made to work for over twelve hours per day and thousands passed on because of exhaust and horrendous working conditions. Starvations brought about by constrained collectivisation, obsolete cultivating rehearses, conveyance chain bungle and above all, resolute disregard of public government assistance killed near 20 million individuals. Millions needed to persevere through loathsome conditions in death camps and not even 50% of those are assessed to have made due. Normal residents needed to carry on with their lives under steady reconnaissance perpetually careful about the guillotine that hung over their heads.

On the other hand, the Soviet organization while being subservient and obsequious to Stalin partook in various advantages and succeeded as a rule in getting around the law. Their oppression on the average folks was unchallenged as long as they obediently toed the partisan principal. In any event, when Stalin was educated with regards to the overabundances of the organization, there is by all accounts no record of any corrective orders gave from the top.

The party which at first developed on Marxist hypotheses during the Tsar time had a great deal of savvy people in its positions whose impact never permitted grouping of party power in a couple of hands. However, since the time Lenin took over Russia, the party bit by bit began losing its majority rule character at the special stepped area of discipline and nationalism. With the rising of Stalin, Lenin's 'vote based centralism' which underlined the unrivaled person of the party authority (Politburo) over others, was to be thoroughly applied. As the years passed, even the Politburo lost its dynamic powers and gave its keys to the General Secretary of the CPSU unequivocally. Absence of balanced governance in organization normally prompted rash and bold independent direction and when the outcomes ended up being sad, the State quickly made unrealistic U-turns submitting much more bumbles during its retreat. Stalin defended his wrongs at whatever point they were out in the open, as 'fundamental annihilation' that would just assistance the nation's advancement over the long haul. If

Fascism stressed racial prevalence over legitimize brutalities like ethnic purging, Stalinism reared on its own baseless fantasies of reliability to defend wanton savagery and persistent man-butcher. As Communism spread across the world in the second 50% of the twentieth century, Stalinism would observe its evil adjust self images in less fortunate nations like China,

Cambodia, and so on However, the Communist Party of the Soviet Union, after the destruction of Stalin didn't keep on being die-hard and presumptuous as was expected.

In 1956, when the remainder of the World had at this point no suspicion of what was unfolding in the USSR, a 60 year-old previous military boss at the twentieth Party Congress in Moscow, would daze the world with a breaking revelation:

'Stalin acted not through influence, clarification and patient participation with individuals, yet by forcing his ideas and requesting outright accommodation to his viewpoint. Whoever went against these ideas or attempted to demonstrate his [own] perspective and the accuracy of his [own] position was ill-fated to expulsion from the administration aggregate and to resulting moral and physical

obliteration. This was particularly obvious during the period following the seventeenth Party Congress, when numerous conspicuous Party pioneers and average Party laborers, legit and committed to the reason for Communism, succumbed to Stalin's oppression'.

The discourse named 'On the Cult of Personality and its Consequences' conveyed by the First Secretary of the CPSU, the accepted head of the USSR would check another takeoff throughout the entire existence of the Empire. Nikita Khrushchev, a veteran who had driven the popular guard of Stalingrad during the Great Patriotic War had rose to the best seven months after Stalin's death. Khrushchev, everything considered, seems, by all accounts, to be the primary head of the USSR who had a bigger number of doubts than haughtiness, more earnestness than obstinacy and generally significant of each of the, a certifiable ability to concede disappointment and gain from botches. That particular mentality, provoked him to convey that age making address that disentangled his archetype openly to the world, and bore declaration to his obligation to uprightness incognizant of the hazardous results that were soon to follow.

THE HEYDAYS

CHAPTER VII

Half Human, Half Beast

Nikita Khrushchev was the child of a helpless worker. He was not profoundly instructed yet was notable for his getting sorted out abilities. His tactical accomplishments had charmed him to Stalin and his closeness to the Dictator was begrudged by a great deal of his partners specifically Malenkov, Beria, and so on Khrushchev, it can't be rejected that he was involved with Stalin's merciless violations during the Great Purges and was instrumental in carrying out a considerable lot of his orders dutifully. He had turned into Stalin's dependable lieutenant after a point and had started to apply his effect on public arrangement making also. Stalin, by mid 1950s was quickly developing feeble and Khrushchev's extreme plans to restore Soviet agribusiness intrigued him a ton. Khrushchev was permitted by Stalin to play out an investigation in a portion of Ukraine's towns called 'The Agrotown Project' which

involved converging of more modest groups into bigger ones for better asset use and expanded efficiency. The analysis bombed seriously and wound up convenient for Khrushchev's opponents to subvert him in the forthcoming power battle. As Stalin's end was becoming inevitable, Malenkov with Beria were caught up with exploring for faithful volunteers inside the party who could be trusted to decide in favor of their camp against that of Khrushchev.

Exorcising Stalin:

Khrushchev then again stayed up with his adversaries going around the nation broadly conveying talks urging masses to zero in on agribusiness. He, inside only a half year after Stalin's passing had figured out how to assemble incredible help from everywhere the country. His goal-oriented venture named Virgin Lands included acquiring large number of sections of land of land Kazakhstan under development to fulfill developing need for food. Despite the fact that there were a lot of blunders in the execution of the undertaking, results were ending up being great. The inventory of grains had developed true to form and Khrushchev's renown rose inside the positions of the party. In the mean time, Malenkov having succeeded Stalin following his demise as the First Secretary of the CPSU, had distinctive long haul plans. He severely needed the party to exit

quickly from the services overseeing different parts of organization. He had plans to maneuver set up technocrats and architects into places of power in order to pulverize red-tapism and restore the vitals of the rusted managerial hardware. Anyway this was not a skilled move thinking about his dubious situation inside the party. The top of the food chain of the CPSU was clearly not ready to free the organization from its long

limbs and thus chose to favor Khrushchev. His garish accomplishment at Virgin Lands humiliated Malenkov appallingly and by September 1953, Khrushchev was casted a ballot to turn into the First Secretary of the CPSU compelling the hapless Malenkov to resign.

Malenkov anyway kept on standing firm on the foothold of Premier with Khrushchev staying the Head of the State. Despite the fact that the two were severe adversaries, the two of them weren't prepared to rehash Stalin's mix-ups. They were consistent in what was called Destalinisation which included exoneration of millions of detainees from inhumane imprisonments and restoration of shamed recent party pioneers. The press was extensively opened up while authors and erudite people were permitted to voice their free suppositions. Despite the fact that its cutoff points were totally encircled, analysis of the public authority, it could securely be said that, was considered the initial time throughout the entire existence of the USSR solely after the development of Khrushchev.

Officials could now enjoy conversations identified with strategy making without the dread of being rebuffed for standing up truly. Khrushchev by 1954, in a milestone move, had chosen to decentralize abilities vested in the Central Presidium permitting town boards and nearby specialists considerable scope in overseeing regulatory issues. Autonomous cultivating was additionally urged by the State to invigorate creation while obtainment costs of grains were climbed impressively. Charges were decreased and measures to alleviate deficiency of purchaser merchandise were executed. The USSR so, inside two or three years after Stalin's demise gradually started to inhale freely.

reformer's travails:

Khrushchev inside a couple of years hosted gained colossal headway inside the get-together outsmarting rivals and solidifying his situation to the degree of driving Premier Malenkov to leave (1956). Khrushchev's transition to activate the satellite countries of the USSR under the Warsaw Pact as a counter hostile to America's NATO was a politically savvy move as it supported the duration of a worldwide bipolarity on the creative mind of millions of colonized individuals who were reeling under the burden of Western Imperialism. Khrushchev's eager Housing Program which permitted various residents to acquire private houses likewise upgraded his standing further. On

February 25 1956, at the twentieth Party Congress, Khrushchev's stunning disclosure of the overabundances submitted during Stalin's time, was a gallant motion which won sincere acclaim from different regions of the planet. Notwithstanding, it would be thoroughly off-base to expect that Khrushchev had a smooth

cruising all through during his initial a long time at the helm.

Khrushchev's stunning reprobation of Stalin made extraordinary distress among the partners of the USSR as it wound up being Moscow's very own open renouncement guessed trustworthiness. It should be recollected that the solidarity of the Eastern Bloc was constructed to a great extent on Kremlin's matchless quality and safeguarding of similar ordered exceptional degrees of cautiousness with respect to the CPSU. It is accounted for that just before the Party Congress, a large portion of his partners were either absolutely ignorant about Khrushchev's arrangements to decry Stalin or were straightforwardly antagonistic to such thoughts frantically encouraging him all an opportunity to drop them. It is accepted that Khrushchev's activities this time was directed by a solid drive of genuineness surfacing out of an annoying inner voice that constrained him to avoid political practicality for a circuitous admission of wrongdoing.

China was the primary nation to transparently communicate disappointment with Moscow's disclosure and Mao, very much like numerous other socialist pioneers began marking Khrushchev as 'revisionist and traditionalist'. Albania broke out of the Cominform that very year while dissenters in Hungary and Poland felt encouraged by Khrushchev's demonstration. In a couple of months, Hungary attempted to break out of the Soviet effective reach however Khrushchev sent his soldiers to crush the defiance as ruthlessly as could be expected. Khrushchev's standard till 1964, as we will see would be described by likewise substituting presentations of altruism and savagery continually helping us to remember his inconcealable Stalinist roots.

A Few Good Men:

J.F.Kennedy when he accepted power in 1961 as the President of the US, was seen to be cut from an alternate fabric from that of his archetypes for his solid radical leanings. Actually like how Khrushchev had frantically needed to split away from the past yet had wound up being its hesitant hostage, Kennedy couldn't resist the urge to surrender to CIA's forceful suggestions regarding Cuba which had as of late turned Communist. Fidel Castro, a youthful and appealling legal counselor turned progressive had figured out how to free Cuba from the grip of US-upheld Franco Batista, the nation's tremendously disdained tyrant in the extended time of 1959. Cuba, for a really long time had been attacked by America's incredible organizations with CIA's assistance however the abrupt rise of Castro in charge had changed things short-term. He banned these partnerships, nationalized all assets, improved training and sponsored medical care. At the point when America forced an exchange ban on Cuba compelling its

partners to take action accordingly, the USSR acted the hero. Exchange between the nations thrived and Communist Cuba endure its tricky infancy.

In April 1962, the CIA with the assistance of Cuban counter-progressives attempted to attack Cuba to depose Castro. Inside three days, the Cuban chief had figured out how to overcome the CIA-upheld powers putting Kennedy to horrendous disgrace. The popular (fizzled) Bay of Pigs Invasion as it is referred to, upgraded Castro's notoriety locally just as globally. Most likely without precedent for history, the chinks in the powerful American defensive layer had been disclosed and the superpower could at this point don't be thought of as totally invulnerable. Castro took the event to manufacture nearer attaches with Moscow to protect his country in case of a future American invasion.

As the years passed, Moscow started to underestimate Cuba and began utilizing the island as its lawn. In the mean time, the US had made plans to utilize Turkey as a base for focusing on Russia and had introduced Jupiter Intercontinental Ballistic Missiles (ICBM) on the Soviet boundaries by 1961. Khrushchev, as a countermeasure, needed to constrain Castro to acknowledge positioning of atomic warheads inside Cuba focusing on the US. The US aviation based armed forces sent covert operative planes over Cuba and affirmed the presence of atomic rockets to the White House. Kennedy had no other decision except for to force a maritime bar around Cuba to stop the inflow of Russian warheads. Strains raised as the Soviet Government informed the White House that a maritime barricade will be treated as nothing under a demonstration of hostility. In a couple of days, line conflicts were accounted for by the Soviet Union and numerous worldwide pioneers were communicating their anxieties toward an all out atomic conflict. Before long Khrushchev's group had to plunk down for arrangements with Kennedy's bureau through a hotline to prevent the contention from getting exacerbated. China's Mao was constraining Khrushchev to proclaim battle in the US while Kennedy's group was likewise eager to take the USSR head-on. Papers all around the world were giving admonition signals about the since quite a while ago feared atomic struggle to which the world out of nowhere had come so close. Messages were passed among Khrushchev and Kennedy consistently while the US military was getting ready for the finale. However it is generally expected revealed that the USSR was in a tough spot as far as atomic strength opposite the US, Khrushchev had been giving tricky signs to the world overstating Russia's potential manifold.

On October 28, 1962, Kennedy got a letter from Khrushchev proposing to pull out the atomic warheads from Cuba, given the former

submitted to eliminate the Jupiter rockets from Turkey and Italy. Lyndon B. Johnson, Kennedy's delegate was not able to take the proposal up while high ranking representatives at Kremlin were frustrated with Khrushchev for having 'flickered first'. It was so great of Khrushchev to have expressed a desire for peace first while it was to the incredible credit of Kennedy to have held onto it promptly to make peace.

The pressure was stopped quickly with the two nations finding a way ways to respect their particular responsibilities while Cuba's power was finally perceived by the US exactly the same year. Regardless of whether Khrushchev was exasperated inside, looking back apparently both the heads of the influence alliances, in any case their political fortunes were sufficiently visionary to remain by harmony and save the world from an incredibly frightful atomic armageddon.

HAPTER VIII

n Unsavory Convergence

One of the main explanations behind me composing this series has been my interest to discover the reason why in the twentieth century both the Satanic Right Wing and the Messianic Left Wing treated the majority the same way despite the fact that their dreams were totally unique. Through my kid venture with

istory, I viewed this inquiry as very interesting to investigate and disentangle, and in the forthcoming pages I will make an honest effort to get to the base of it.

Theoretical Foundations of the Right:

To discover what underlies the Right wing of the political range, we will examine Nordicism, a racial hypothesis proliferated by the Nazis. This hypothesis is emphatically based upon the establishment of the inborn matchless quality of the White/Nordic/Aryan Race and a solid conviction that a general public is 'just and regular' provided that it complies with the antiquated changeless laws of endurance. Actually like how the lions are at the highest point of the natural way of life in a wilderness, the Aryans reserve each option to rule and improve themselves at the expense of the lesser races. The lesser races are called along these lines, since they are made of mediocre characteristics like misleading, taking, pitiful appearances and such, and contact of the prevalent races with them will bring about tainting prompting loss of 'racial virtue'. If there arises a condition where mixing of races is unavoidable (as in private enterprise), a total cleanse of the lesser races is prescribed and as indicated by old laws, such demonstrations of 'ethnic purifying' are totally justified.

As you can see, the Right imagines a future 'perfect world' where mastery of

a gathering of people over the other is only the rule that everyone must follow, truth be told of that of Nature, and a general public which has inconsistent admittance to assets isn't just inescapable yet additionally fundamental for the improvement of the human condition. Individuals who have a solid faith in these qualities, who consider antagonist convictions as nothing not as much as 'heresy' and consequently stay impenetrable and threatening to them, are frequently called 'fundamentalists'.

Every general public which is under motion, at a given moment of time, will have both Right-wing or Conservative components and a totally contradictory arrangement of Left-Wing components whose shared cooperation or struggle is the thing that we call the advancement of human progress. The Church of the fifteenth century which unequivocally mishandled Copernicus for his Helio-driven model of the Universe can without much of a stretch be

delegated the Right Wing of the middle age Europe while current creators like him who tested conventional conviction frameworks with logical clarifications can be marked 'Moderate or The Left'.

Needless to say, the provincial desires of the Industrial West were firmly supported by Right Wing convictions and the subjugated people groups of Africa and Asia were additionally made to have faith in them. Likewise, the strict conventionality of these slave countries was additionally generally, either unaffected by the frontier abundances or completely strong of it. The extremely uninvolved job of the Hindu Right in India's battle for freedom serves to epitomize this.

Theoretical Foundations of the Left:

Karl Marx, then again imagined a future where there is basically no double-dealing of one man by the other, where every individual distinguishes himself with the remainder of the general public and where one's goals and requirements exist in ideal congruity with that of the entirety. We consider such a future a Communist Utopia where no man is viewed as over the other. Marx was intensely motivated by the Paris Commune trial of 1871 and expounded broadly on its significance to contemporary society. His works spread

during the mid twentieth century and set off developments across the world both in the Industrial West and the colonized East.

The decision classes all around the world whose mastery was blessed by Right Wing speculations had sufficient motivation to feel frightened. India's political dissidents of the pre Gandhian period like Dadabhai Naoroji, Motilal Nehru were straightforwardly impacted by global moderate developments which moved them to build a thorough evaluate of expansionism whose establishments laid not completely on feelings of patriotism, but rather significantly on the financial thought processes basic government. These leaders

were instrumental in the development of the Indian National Congress in 1885 which in years and years was to transform into one of the biggest mass associations on the planet. In 1927, Brussels in Belgium facilitated a meeting known as the League Against Imperialism that comprised of heads of different colonized countries meeting up to challenge Western authority in Asia (Jawaharlal Nehru was India's agent) and Africa in a solitary, bound together voice. The League was coordinated and upheld by Communist Russia and in numerous ways, it filled in as the forerunner to the Non Aligned Movement of 1961 that brought a large portion of the past states under one umbrella.

Leninism vs Marxism:

Communist systems of the twentieth century, it can easily be asserted that they were all tyrant in different degrees, from the disgustingly merciless Stalin's system to a tolerably severe one in Tito's Yugoslavia. Thus, even somebody who has solid socialist tendencies are driven into the end that both socialism and autocracy are absolutely indivisible. Anyway one should recall that since the greater part of the nations of the last century turned socialist under solid Soviet impact and needed to depend on tyrants like Stalin for their endurance, suppression was inescapable in all nations. This empowers us to promptly expect that socialism might have been more agreeable world over had the Soviet Union not been excessively nosy into the issues of different nations. In any case, it truly was not generally so straightforward as that.

Pol Pot, the socialist head of Cambodia killed a large number of residents during his short time of rule (1975-79) without even a bit of rationale. It should be recalled that there was certifiably not an extensive impact of Soviet Union during the development of Communist Cambodia and henceforth exceptionally less motivation to turn severe. China also presents an extremely fascinating situation where Mao, the originator head of the nation despite the fact that he was viewed as a theoretician and a free mastermind much the same as Vladimir Lenin, on whom the impact of Stalin must be immaterial, likewise stayed a dictator during most piece of his standard. His trials like the Great Leap Forward and the Cultural Revolution, however they had respectable intentions wound up gulping the existences of millions of its residents. At the foundation of these investigations, the insidious expectation to succeed was exacerbated by a total dismissal for living souls. More cases like Romania, Poland, East Germany, Ukraine present comparable peculiarities however levels of suppression shift extraordinarily in every last one of them.

So we at last consider that a socialist framework to be far as it has existed has

flourished distinctly under states of viciousness and restraint and this leads us to address even the authenticity of the Marxist convention itself. Marx, in his works had vouched for a short 'tyranny of the low class' during the Socialist period of the Revolution. By tyranny he implied the standard of the common laborers over the propertied classes which would improve the creation relations of a general public to improve things. Marx additionally had allocated the authority of the Revolution to the Communist Party which was to fill in as the 'vanguard of the working class'. The Party should teach the majority, radicalize the worker's guilds and laborer associations lastly lead the battle against the propertied classes.

However, when we investigate what occurred in Russia, we observe that Lenin had really done the opposite. Initially, the term 'fascism' was taken in a real sense and the expression 'vanguard of the working class' appallingly confused. The 'vanguard of the working class' really implied a gathering of people who best address the adaptable interests of the average workers which decide the speed and the course of the Revolution. An initiative which doesn't consider the goals of the working class has no option to call itself 'the vanguard'. This normally implies that the Communist Party, the sole delegate of the regular workers, should work justly, support discuss and adequately decentralize authority. In any case, what Lenin had made was a cadre of top party individuals whose elitism was strikingly show in what was called 'majority rule centralism'. The party first class or the Politburo took choices all alone, passed orders descending and constrained party individuals to go along. Nonconformists were convinced over and over to acknowledge the partisan principal or to leave the association by and large. The Politburo had such a lot of haughtiness for the general population that it accepted that the majority had no personalities of their own and that it was its bounden obligation to teach and guide them to a superior future.

Democratic Centralism which was a fundamental piece of Leninism was consequently a horrendous mutilation of the Marxist hypothesis. This sort of training was spread to every one of the satellites of the USSR and different nations too. When Stalin accepted power, he applied the hypothesis thoroughly on the Soviet society and collected abhorrent results.

Simultaneously, he likewise debilitated the Politburo by moving power into himself and passed on his replacements to acquire the same.

Origins of Tyranny:

Hitler during his early stages had drenched himself in dubious hypotheses of prejudice and when he climbed to the highest point of the Nazi party, he was at that point a persuaded conservative. He trusted in the mutilated translations of Nietzsche and Darwin and had needed to purify the general public of the impurities of substandard races. He truly despised Marxism which had vouched for all inclusive fraternity and felt that it was totally against the Order of Nature. Individuals like Hitler who here and there are influenced by hypotheses that sound like 'a definitive truth' mentally are leaned to accept immovably in their own 'unrivaled' insight. Their dreams are entirely solid and inebriating, to the point that they will generally consider others oblivious and here and there even unnecessary. A comparative examination can be attracted to left wingers who have ventured out into Marxist hypothesis. Communism, as it is broadly noticed, is an astoundingly logical hypothesis that deciphers the entire of mankind's set of experiences in a serious significant manner and gives you the apparatuses to shift its future direction. It is actually the case that Marxism opens your windows to a wide assortment of disciplines that any Marxist researcher will see it hard to land from this very freeing scholarly excursion. Really out of my own encounters, I unequivocally feel that Marxism gives you a dream of 'a definitive truth' and it is very regular that youthful, rich personalities are immediately stricken by it. Anyway the most concerning issue emerges when one accidentally views himself as the Chosen One to understand Marx's vision of Communist Utopia actually like how legendary texts here and there energize a clueless brain into an attack of aficionado euphoria.

It is definitively at that point, the understudy of Marxism transforms into a fundamentalist by becoming impenetrable to any sort of antagonist convictions. The facts confirm that our understudy finds elevated aims to carry harmony and flourishing to every last one, rather than his traditional partner who has confidence in the legitimacy of a broke society, however that doesn't make him any less a fundamentalist. Any sort of fundamentalism quickly breeds prejudice and contempt anticipating a miserable acquiescence of the remainder of the world towards it. At the point when dissidents like us have no compunctions in calling conservatives as 'biased people' and 'extremists', it is unexpected to take note of that we don't show similar status to mark Marxist supremacists like Lenin, Stalin with similar labels. At the point when a specific gathering views itself as higher than the remainder of the general public and looks for authenticity of its clout because of it, it should be marked 'extremist' regardless of whether its aims are probably honorable. Furthermore, any sort of autocracy, be it strict or scholarly for this situation, intrinsically harbors a hatred towards the blameless masses which transforms soon into dictatorship whose results are

wherever to see.

HAPTER IX

n Unceremonious End

The world was staggered on October 4, 1957. No nation of the primary world had figured out how to accomplish this accomplishment. Another age had been proclaimed by as a matter of fact the "retrograde commies'. There was very little festival in the CPSU organ Pravda to coordinate with the degree of shock and caution that sprinkled all around the title texts of Western papers. At the point when the Russians had wrecked the Nazis in 1945 to seal a great triumph over the Axis powers, the Western world had been clubbed into an unassuming affirmation of the Soviet military may. In any event, when the Soviet Union was advancing with huge paces of monetary development during the mid 1930s, particularly when the remainder of the world was wrestling with negative paces of development inferable from the Depression, the West wasn't exactly charmed with regards to the inquisitive viability of the Soviet Model. Yet, before the Second's over World War, for the Western Elite there was no getting away from the way that there for sure was one more superpower, this time from the Eastern area of the planet. However, inside twenty years of that excellent accomplishment, the USSR had figured out how to strike once more, this time precisely at the core of the Western pride. Sputnik 1, the very first man-made satellite was dispatched effectively into the space from Baikonur, Kazakh ASSR by the Soviet Space Agency. The First Secretary of the CPSU, the then top of the Soviet State, Nikita Khrushchev was named 'Man Of the Year 1957' by TIME magazine the equivalent year.

Goo of good intentions:

Khrushchev needed to build the country's horticultural creation complex and guarantee independence, by overwhelmingly extending his pet Virgin Lands Experiment. He needed to redirect the humongous measure of assets going into the protection spending plan towards agrarian and modern development. To limit safeguard spending, he made a special effort to warm up to the United States. He got researchers from Iowa the U.S to the USSR to set up corn fields and boost corn creation. He expanded expenses for manure and pesticide fabricating and escalated his examination on food creation. He opened Party gatherings and gatherings to the general population and requested scattering of the procedures through papers and different media. To top everything, he split the party structure into two - one to administer farming and the other to control industry.

Khrushchev by 1958, had figured out how to assume responsibility for the whole party by

debilitating the situation of Stalinist pioneers. He dismissed Bulganin and eliminated any individual who disrupted the general flow of his benevolent change. He changed party laws as to supplant panel individuals intermittently at all levels of the association. He likewise worked intensely on the recovery of 'shamed' party men and authorities who fell under Stalin's radar during the Great Terror. Yet, the saddest piece of the story was that none of these moves wound up yielding expected results.

The Virgin Lands project, inside a range of five years could presently don't support the attractive yields that it produced at first. By mid 1960s, the undertaking was ending up being a disappointment with quickly lessening returns. His driven corn task and his moves to patch up dairy industry were additionally not working because of administrative idiocy and ill-advised preparation. His extreme dependence on a hereditary researcher Lysenko whose questionable accreditations came out just later, for working on the nature of yield ended up being an immense mix-up. Khrushchev's public reprobation of Stalin disillusioned large numbers of his own allies in the party and accidentally induced the development of many amazing opponent groups. In particular, the bifurcation of the party association made totally unanticipated issues. A large portion of the party frameworks working under Khrushchev were not the sort of submitted optimists who shaped the bedrock of the party during Lenin's time. Since the time Stalin's cleanses, the piece of the party had been enormously modified with careerists, sharks and controllers supplanting those caring partymen and past progressives who had up until recently involved higher positions. Khrushchev's arrangements to occasionally supplant 33% of the unit had scratched the possibilities of them arriving at the higher rungs of the association while his extreme move to part the party into two was hated profoundly nearly at all levels. Officially as well, the bifurcation was an extraordinary calamity because of an unavoidable covering of obligations between the agribusiness and industry verticals which thusly prompted a great deal of duplication of capacities and tasks.

Finally, Khrushchev's transition to accommodate with Kennedy during the Missile Crisis of 1962 was likewise not valued by numerous individuals of the party's hardliners and his recent allies. He was before long segregated inside by his antagonized associates who were hanging tight for a chance to eliminate him from power.

'I won't put up a fight'

Nikita Khrushchev's way to deal with different countries was totally in opposition to that of his archetype. He restored relations with Marshal Tito of Yugoslavia despite the fact that the last option was very hesitant to reconcile.

Khrushchev's significant assistance to China to construct its own atomic innovation was likewise not adequately responded by Mao. China had some time before casted off the Soviet way to deal with Socialism and attempted to develop its own model dedicating it 'Communism with Chinese qualities'. In the Indochina emergency including the United States, Khrushchev needed to go delicate and slow to keep away from enormous scope military conflicts while Mao stayed cold and enduring. China's forceful disposition stressed Khrushchev frightfully and he was pushed to the mark of unexpectedly pulling out all specialized help and gear for the finish of the goal-oriented Chinese atomic mission. This was on the grounds that, Khrushchev trusted that an unrestricted Mao, particularly at the tallness of the Indochina emergency would maneuver the whole world into an atomic conflict and consequently he did his absolute best to alleviate the circumstance. He wouldn't fret drawing analysis from his associates and East European partners when he visited the United States in 1959 to turn into the principal Soviet pioneer to do as such. He additionally met J.F.Kennedy at Vienna in 1961 to determine both the Indochina and Berlin issues amicably.

regardless of his earnest attempts to chop down military use through dealings and compromises with the U.S, the circumstance in Vietnam and Laos deteriorated during his years negatively affecting the general Soviet monetary wellbeing. As his undertakings at extending agribusiness through enormous state ventures were fizzling without creating comparable returns, the USSR needed to depend on different nations for food to determine regular deficiencies and starvations that were as a rule progressively revealed the nation over. His choice to climb the costs of food articles because of deficiencies in 1962 prompted dissents wherever which must be put down forcibly.

n October 14, 1964, Leonid Brezhnev driving an incredible group of top pioneers reinforced by guaranteed support from all levels of the party, coordinated an upset effectively, by capturing Khrushchev quickly upon his return from get-away, inside the premises of the Moscow air terminal itself. At the point when Khrushchev was stood up to by KGB authorities, he immediately comprehended the circumstance and co-worked with them without raising cries of protest.

Inspite of such countless downfalls and mix-ups, the one who was basically answerable for the De-Stalinisation of the country in the midst of fermenting political resistance, the kind tyrant who figured out how to work on the expectations for everyday comforts of his residents with his massively effective lodging plan, the principal head of the USSR who put stock in quiet conjunction with neighbors and opponents, the perplexing Nikita Khrushchev, left the scene

subsequent to filling in as the Head of the State for quite some time. It has been accounted for that Khrushchev called his partner Anastas Mikoyan during the very night after his ouster and talked the accompanying words:

"I'm old and tired. Allow them to adapt without help from anyone else. I've done the primary concern. Could anybody have longed for let Stalin know that he sometimes fell short for us any longer and proposing he resign? Not so much as a wet spot would have remained where we had been standing. Presently everything is unique. The dread is gone, and we can talk as equivalents. That is my commitment. I will not set up a fight."

CHAPTER X

mells of Autumn

Alexei Kosygin turned into the Prime Minister (Chairman of the Council of Ministers) in 1964 promptly following Brezhnev's increase to the top. Kosygin was a technocrat and the new authority showed a solid enthusiasm to change the public business through specialized development and reasonable authoritative re-association. Different parts of the business were permitted adequate elbowroom to associate among themselves which Kosygin thought would inject some dynamism into the cycles of creation. This move ordered some measure of decentralization since the State needed to pull out of the matter of setting creation targets. Value controls were tolerably loose and request arranged targets instead of Stating commanded ones were presented. The idea of execution based motivation was extended to a wide range of enterprises. The change presented in 1965, required around five years to get executed in full and prospects of worked on monetary result and better ways of life looked bright.

Costs of Being the Saviour:

Inspite of going against gauges from different sources, we can securely expect that the USSR was allotting in excess of 25% of its yearly financial plan towards military costs post the downfall of Stalin. In the post WW2 period, particularly after Khrushchev assumed control over, the USSR was simply glad to support the requirements of the Third World, loaning monetary and military help to different enemy of provincial developments against the West. However, during Brezhnev's period the contention between the Western powers and the Vietnamese Communists had heightened and the USSR was obliged to support the last option's mission, completely. The North Vietnamese volunteer army was driven by Ho Chi Minh who banked vigorously on the help of the Soviet Union both during the First Indochina battle against the supreme France and furthermore during the Second Indochina War, otherwise called the Vietnam War,

against the United States-drove powers. The conflict which went on for over 10 years was one of the bloodiest ever, with Vietnam being beat by multiple occasions the absolute ammo utilized by every one of the belligerents in the Second World War. Despite the fact that the conflict depleted the American economy impressively, the Soviet Union by mid 1970s is accounted for to have spent near 7 billion USD to help Communist Vietnam stand and battle on its own legs. As the conflict attracted to a nearby in 1975 with the loss of the American powers, the esteem of the Soviet Union as a veritable military superpower, ascended higher among the world countries, despite the fact that it was bought at a horribly unreasonable expense to the inner economy.

The Soviets helped in the unification of the entire of Vietnam under Ho Chi Minh, additionally drawing the more modest countries like Cambodia and Laos into the recently framed Southeast Asian Communist alliance. Brezhnev, despite the fact that a Stalinist by rule, was not ready to leave Khrushchev's endeavors to restore homegrown horticulture and industry, because of which earnest drives, for example, Kosygin's changes were carried out under his system. The Soviet society which went through a gigantic industrialisation drive under Stalin (to the detriment of agribusiness) stayed a roaring economy until the last part of the 1960s, the specific place of enunciation in its monetary direction where the expenses of the Cold War were starting to gradually disintegrate the establishments of the youthful economy. Additionally Brezhnev drove the Soviet atomic program to its obvious end result by immensely putting resources into the innovation and by the mid 1970s, even favorable to Western spectators hesitantly recognized that the Soviet Union had accomplished its most pined for atomic equality with the United States.

Yet, the way that the USSR stayed home to great many starved individuals who needed to stand by in long lines to acquire their fundamental necessities for their everyday endurance was totally irrefutable. These real factors coincided with the way that by the mid 1970s, the USSR had developed right around 60% to the size of the US economy. However, from that point on, Brezhnev's standard up to the breakdown of the Empire under Gorbachev in 1991, was described by monetary stagnation and ensuing decline.

'You are not him'

A ton of reasons could be credited to the stagnation and continuous decay of the Soviet economy, one of which was the idea of the Communist Party authority that triumphed ultimately the final say regarding all parts of the nation's organization. As referenced before, the party piece particularly at the top of the pyramid was comprised of force mongers, careerists and surprisingly dark advertisers during Brezhnev's time. The incredible progressive vision shaped and sustained during Lenin and Stalin's time was totally forgotten during the 1970s and all endeavors were focused on holding power to the extent that this would be possible. Accordingly, the aggressive changes of Kosygin were extensively weakened during the execution stage with the Party authorities proceeding to beat industry directors in the dynamic regions identified with material stream, organic market the board. Directors and higher authorities controlled the impetus framework so well that they accomplished sensational modifications in their yearly compensation consistently, while the remainder of the specialists were passed on to wrestle with expanding costs and deteriorating compensation. Roads to advance were likewise not adequately investigated since there were severe cutoff points on R&D ventures and extremely negligible prizes and motivators for fruitful developments. Indeed, even market-based interest conditions to the degree it was permitted to exist couldn't achieve enhancements in the nature of buyer items that arrived at the end user.

Secondly, the Soviet Union saw enormous movement of residents from provincial to metropolitan regions right from the times of Stalin and by the last part of the 1970s, the metropolitan populace nearly overwhelmed the absolute number of rustic occupants. The majority of the metropolitan residents were modern specialists, representatives, office conveyors and educators whose interest for buyer items was developing quickly year-on-year. These requests couldn't be met by the stock chains oversaw by the State which normally gave way to a flourishing dark economy. Despite the fact that its size stays a secret to everybody, the effect of the underground market on the existences of metropolitan residents was exceptionally enormous. The presence of the underground market and its relentless development stood declaration to the vast openings in the rusting Soviet order driven financial model which was then again being enormously depleted by the Cold War costs.

What's more another most significant component that sabotaged the Soviet economy was the massive franticness that educated the demeanor regarding its authority towards financial preparation, about the need to rival the United States and remain applicable all the time in the urgent philosophical fight. A prevalently agrarian Russia of the 1920s need not have been, at the primary spot push into a horrifying industrialisation drive under Stalin that too at such a humongous human and material expense. Also the irritating uncertainty of the authority that pushed them to every now and again contrast the financial marks of Russia and that of the United States blocked any useful

endeavor to earnestly study and address the developing requests of its enduring residents. According to my own perspective, it's anything but a slip-up to accept that the United States was a profoundly industrialized country right from the 1920s and financial development of the superpower post the Second World War was headed generally, by draining the hapless Third World economies spread across Latin America, Africa and Asia. Then again, from sources considered solid, it could unhesitatingly be expressed that the Soviet Union didn't colonize or take advantage of its East European satellites however much its Western partner did in the asset rich Third World. Soviet Russia, likely attributable to its optimistic roots gave more than whatever it took from the remainder of the world and a large portion of its monetary accomplishments were made conceivable, in contrast to its rival, not due to its forceful expansionism world over, however completely inspite of it. Soviet assistance to Communist China in its early stages is safely assessed to surpass 4 billion USD as per different sources while its monetary guide to Cuba and more youthful socialist countries like Vietnam, Cambodia, and so on is accepted to have moved toward practically a similar aggregate. Obviously, these were gigantic exchanges of abundance from the USSR to the Third World that were driven generally by altruism and philosophical responsibility that effectively superseded business and geo-political considerations.

It is another basic yet essential reality that appears to have escaped the arrangement creators of the Soviet Union that their economy was not displayed to make due on benefit thought processes and flourish with attendant radical plans, in contrast to that of the United States and thus, correlations of financial development rates between the two nations will undoubtedly be worthless and frequently exceptionally misleading.

However, the 'Destalinised' Soviet Union having been changed into an impressive superpower endowed with 'super' obligations which it couldn't manage bearing over the long haul, soldiered on through the 1970s consistently and uncomplainingly with a courageous face. In 1979, Leonid Brezhnev, this time got a call for help from adjoining Afghanistan administered by a group ridden Communist Party to set its home all together as fast as could really be expected. The Soviet Politburo that met on December 24, 1979 at Moscow without its Premier Kosygin, hesitantly requested the quick sending of troops to Afghanistan. The thickly eye browed Brezhnev leaned back on his seat in one of the stale smelling rooms of the Kremlin probably thought that it is difficult to cover the developing kinks of stress that were quickly spreading all over his

temple, before long he had marked the request. Had the uncannily versatile Soviet Union oversaw finally, to find a fresher street to its destruction?

CHAPTER XI

he Beginning of Autumn

In 1968, the public authority drove by the Communist Party of Czechoslovakia endeavored to change the economy through market arranged measures yet stringently inside the domain of communism by empowering laborer cooperatives and market valuing rules. Opportunity of articulation was likewise energized which incited the majority to request better wages and working conditions. Alexander Dubcek, the then Head of the Czechoslovakian state started these changes against the desires of the Party universality. Dubcek was cautioned a few times by Moscow to pull out the changes with quick impact, while regular citizen fights started to spread all around the nation quickly. Dubcek would not move in any event, when different countries of the Warsaw Pact compressed him to withdraw. Following a couple of days, Leonid Brezhnev chose to send troops into Prague to put down the revolt. The changes were moved back and Czechoslovakia was shown its spot in the East European camp. The Prague Spring of 1968, as it is broadly called was instrumental in the detailing of the Brezhnev Doctrine, an understanding which enabled Moscow to meddle into the inward undertakings of its satellites at whatever point a danger to communist dependability and harmony was detected.

The Soviet Citizen:

The USSR had finished over sixty years of communism by the 1970s and just about several ages of individuals had been conceived and raised in the progressive Soviet climate. The severe idea of the State had during Brezhnev's time been altogether changed and individuals could figure out how to have quiet existences as long as they didn't screw with the public authority. The Russian residents, a larger part of them however poor by the guidelines of the West, were guaranteed of free instruction and medical services, occupations and work benefits regardless of whether they needed to line awake for hours to purchase their every day basics. There were no significant starvations or huge scope deficiencies of food in the Union post-Khrushchev and most Russians ate sparingly if worse and craving, it could securely be said was unmistakably a thing of the Stalinist past. The functioning states of modern and rural work were definitely less harsh than they were during the early stages of the Union and thus getting acquainted with them was a sorry stretch for the majority of the Russians. An impressive piece of the labor force was made of overcomers of the Stalinist

request and henceforth they fared much better during the long stretches of Brezhnev. The social existence of the Russians under Brezhnev was portrayed by tremendous film lobbies including antiquated dramas, purposeful publicity motion pictures, melodies and sound plays communicated by the State claimed radio. Since there was very little extension for assortment diversion in Russia and furthermore on the grounds that a significant part of the general population was educated, the Russians had a uniquely developed perusing propensity that developed especially after Khrushchev's period of Destalinisation. Russians could get to scholarly works of art from around the world and those books from the West which described anecdotes about lavish individuals and more liberated social orders were likewise permitted. From an assortment of recorded sources, it has been borne out that during Brezhnev's period, Russia was the second biggest economy on the planet and furthermore the biggest maker of steel, pig iron, concrete and farm haulers. The Union, in equal was additionally sponsoring a ton of more youthful countries shunned by the remainder of the world. Notwithstanding these accomplishments, the way that they had been the initial ones to enter space was additionally an issue of incredible pride for the Russian commoners.

hough there have been a ton of inconsistent reports on this, there is a ton of proof that during Brezhnev's time, the Russians, inspite of holding onto a lot of feelings of resentment against the organization had the option to adjust to live calmly under the iron fisted communist state and even have satisfied existences. Regardless of whether the veracity of these confirmations could be addressed, it must be conceded that a ton of domains of the past, regardless of whether they were considered enormous and awkward to control, had figured out how to endure longer than one would normally accept, not entirely through effective contraptions of suppression and publicity, yet additionally to a huge measure, by getting incredible qualities from the supernatural strength of their subjects and their marvelous sense for endurance. Yet, Brezhnev's Russia, not normal for that of his archetypes was undeniably not so much harsh but rather more welfarist and henceforth it becomes more straightforward to trust when one of the new reviews held post-Soviet Russia presumed that Brezhnev was the most famous head of the Soviet century.

Reagan's masterstroke:

Leonid Brezhnev, after a delayed ailment kicked the bucket on November 10, 1982 in the wake of administering the USSR for near eighteen years. Post his destruction, shockingly there was no power battle without precedent for the historical backdrop of the state and another sexagenarian chief Yuri Andropov succeeded him. He before long was supplanted by Konstantin Chernenko in the wake of being in power for near fifteen months. Under Chernenko the USSR boycotted the 1984 Summer

Olympics held at Los Angeles in fitting reaction to the US blacklist of the 1980 Moscow Olympics. 73-year old Chernenko who burned through the majority of his residency in medical clinic getting therapy passed on in February 1985. Chernenko's destruction provided Soviet Union with its most youthful Head of State ever, Mikhail Gorbachev who was essential for the new reformist gatekeeper of the Party.

On the other hand, Ronald Reagan was chosen as the President of the United States in 1981. Reagan, frequently thought to be a curve moderate was not ready to proceed with his archetype Jimmy Carter's appeasing disposition towards the Soviets. During the Oil Glut of 1981, he could see that falling worldwide oil costs could debilitate the monetary establishments of the USSR since a significant part of Soviet income was subject to its oil trades. The Soviet mediation in Afghanistan was generally financed by Russia's monstrous oil fields and Reagan was of the assessment that if the worldwide circumstance would be exacerbated by expanded American spending on the Cold War, on the occasion of an unexpected fall in global oil costs the Soviet economy would immediately implode and go to a crushing stop. Of course, Reagan quickly requested escalation of American association in different nations across the globe like Yemen, Libya, Angola, Indonesia,etc by mixing billions of dollars into intermediary wars backing conservative oppressive systems and favorable to Western aggressor outfits against nearby Communists and freedom developments. Reagan's move in 1986 to supply the Afghan Mujahideens with the most recent Stinger Anti - Aircraft rocket denoted a significant turning point for the Islamists who were trapped in an apparently wearisome conflict with the Soviet army.

In 1986, the Saudi Arabian pioneers reported their choice to expand the development of oil to cut the costs down. There is some proof that the CIA constrained the Saudis to impact such a move as a feature of Reagan's enemy of Soviet system. True to form, global oil costs tumbled and the USSR in practically no time, experienced a horrible asset crunch. Gorbachev had for some time been a quiet pundit of the Brezhnev Doctrine and right from his long periods of accepting office, he was thinking about ways of racking it for the last time. His emphasis was on working on homegrown modern creation by utilizing the most recent accessible innovation and bettering the expectations for everyday comforts of the Russians. He understood that the Union was spending near a fourth of its GDP towards military costs still up in the air to put his foot down at the earliest opportunity. The Oil Shock of 1986 rushed his choice to pull out from

the conflict in Afghanistan against the restored Mujahideens and by 1988, the Soviets started to withdraw in stages passing on Kabul's PDPA-ledgovernment to fight for itself.

Gorbachev needed to acknowledge that the Soviet misfortune in Afghanistan had been a horrendous embarrassment for the incredible realm however he trusted that there were far greater humiliations to manage. Without precedent for Soviet history, the yearly financial development during the 1980s was moving toward nothing, seriously taking steps to go negative. Reagan's ploy had worked and Gorbachev needed to make something appear out of nowhere quickly to endure the moment.

In 1987 after the Chernobyl atomic fiasco, the USSR under a unique Gorbachev reported another arrangement of strategies specifically, 'glasnost' and 'perestroika', which in a real sense implied receptiveness and change. In contrast to that of his archetypes, this time the term 'change' was implied genuinely. Gorbachev conflicted with the assessments of his associates to get them carried out on the ground as fast as could really be expected. Therefore, inside several years, Gorbachev's perestroika had the option to create not just unmistakable social outcomes and obvious financial results yet in addition unexpected and surprisingly dangerous outcomes that would ultimately linger up to gulp down the entire of the Soviet Empire itself.

THE INDIAN CONNECTION

Before we branch out to explore the climactic periods of the Soviet breakdown, I truly consider it basic to analyze the job of Soviet enlivened communist developments in India whose effect on our political and public activities can barely be overstated. The Soviet Union, it should be recalled, was an amazing impact over the spaces it politically controlled as well as over terrains and areas which scarcely knew just its name.

One such nation was India whose course in history was emphatically attached to that of the Soviet Union and whose complicated relationship with the last option requests a definite assessment that should length something like two sections from here.

CHAPTER XII

he Socialist South

The primary part will zero in on the South where the Soviet impact was generally more articulated while different parts will attempt to give a skillet Indian record of the occasions. This section has extra accentuation on Tamilnadu's legislative issues for clear reasons.

The October Revolution in Russia prevailed in 1917. The Communist Party of India was framed precisely eight years after the fact. Socialist thoughts spread like quickly and communists multiplied all over India during the 1930s roused by the huge steps made by the Soviet Union's order economy. Jawaharlal Nehru drove an exceptionally persuasive group of Soviet-propelled left wingers inside the Congress party itself. The Congress in 1938 additionally took on a goal to follow a Soviet-style arranged monetary model once the British Raj was discarded. E.V.Ramaswami, a social reformer who proceeded to lead the most compelling 'Dravidian development' in Tamilnadu got going as a socialist in the mid 1920s. The term Revolution which until now had not been essential for well known speech anyplace began turning into a family word all over India. Whatever was intended to address a new thing and way breaking was given a 'progressive' prefix.

Congress Socialism:

Post-Independence, the main common decisions held in Madras State gave a reasonable command to a Communist - drove coalition. Notwithstanding a demonstration of treachery by the veteran Congressman C.Rajagopalachari, the Communists would have headed the primary common administration of Madras Presidency. Notwithstanding, that occasion could cause no harm to the developing allure of communist thoughts all over South India. The Congress Government drove by Kamaraj from 1954 followed a government assistance model giving prime significance to the development of schooling and production of public area ventures. Regular assets were nationalized, government funded schools with noontime feast conspire were opened everywhere, public dispersion framework to rearrange grain was made and fortified. In equal, the Dravidian ideologues who overwhelmed the statures of the thriving Tamil film industry guaranteed that the 'common' components of the general public were related to the Congress party overall and depicted the party in helpless light through films that spoke to the nationalistic pride of Tamil speakers. Similar to Soviet publicity films that typically showed plotting landowners and aristocrats being bested eventually by devastated laborers, Tamil film too agitated social dramatizations, verifiable movies that shed light on the predicament of the workers, ladies took advantage of by rich men and property managers, strict godmen abusing the confidence of the devotees to accumulate fortunes, etc.

Trade associations for the most part subsidiary to the Communist factions spread across modern towns and left-wing worker social orders that battled rank, class and sex disparities increased across rustic South India. Aggressor left wing bunches multiplied across Kerala and Telangana areas particularly where position double-dealing was at its pinnacle. Upper standing landowners whose excesses

stayed unchecked by progressive Congress legislatures were disposed of by Communist extremist gatherings and land rearrangement programs were executed. At the point when EMS Namboodiripad headed the world's first fairly chose Communist Government in Kerala in 1957, a huge land change program to dispense with rank and class abuse was dispatched. Kerala's schooling which was up until recently overwhelmed via land-possessing Christian universality was brought under the domain of the State Government. In the interim grounds under Hyderabad Nizam's suzerainty were freed by Communist assailants and rearranged to Telangana peasants.

Communists lose to 'Socialism':

In 1967, a left wing alliance government headed by the DMK deposed the Congress Government in Tamilnadu and started one more round of government assistance measures. Land change was carried out (whose pace of achievement was entirely problematic) without precedent for Tamilnadu. Hindu sanctuaries that possessed tremendous sections of land of land were nationalized, essential training framework was reinforced and a large number of redistributive plans were started. The more the DMK moved leftward in the political range inspite of widespread organized defilement, the more underestimated the standard socialist coalitions became in Tamilnadu. Their discretionary fortunes consistently dwindled as the DMK before long split into two, leading to a more up to date coalition drove by film whiz MG Ramachandran in 1972. MGR, as he was lovingly called was the banner kid of the Dravidian development right from its days as a mass association. Quite possibly the main reason why Tamilnadu turned leftward moving increasingly more along Dravidian lines was the ubiquity of MGR whose public picture was assembled emphatically around the thoughts of communism and libertarianism. He regularly played in his movies, the hero of the common laborers who had the uncommon guts to scrutinize the abhorrent landowners and other ravenous personal stakes. The vast majority of his tunes that outlasted his time had incredible music and group satisfying social messages which assumed a basic part in dispersing Dravidian purposeful publicity among the majority. As referenced before, the Dravidian development promoted calling more current and extremist things 'progressive' expecting to take a portion of the enchantment the October Revolution had made across the world and MGR was called 'progressive pioneer' by his fans on his street to turning into the main film star to get chosen as the Chief Minister of a state in 1977.

he split of the DMK into two prompted two significant sweeping outcomes. One, the nature of Soviet roused welfarism soon deteriorated

into turning into a model of debasement driven populism where individuals were consistently kept in the bondage of destitution while at the same time being taken care of with a large number of State supported gifts that went from food-grains to customer durables. Two, with the presence of fresher entertainers in Tamilnadu legislative issues, the standard Left contracted frightfully losing tremendous lumps of its appointive help to its pseudo-communist opponents. The Left anyway kept on overwhelming mass associations, for example, worker's organizations and laborer social orders because of which laborers and ranchers in Tamilnadu figured out how to accomplish sensible ways of life through nonstop battles for better wages and everyday environments.

oribund communism:

As the century moved closer to a nearby, Tamilnadu attributable to its progressive welfarist state run administrations drove by both the Dravidian parties had better than expected proficiency rates, better streets and foundation and nice wellbeing norms, all of which came in great stead, when in 1991, India moved towards a market-driven modern economy. Worldwide companies which saw modest work in India floated more towards the South than the North for need of better specialized abilities and organized proficient training to build up plants, programming improvement focuses, trade handling units,etc in its tremendous all around kept up with metropolitan regions. Urban areas like Chennai, Bangalore, Coimbatore developed into modern center points under the aegis of the State in this way giving admirably paying positions to a large number of individuals who thus moved quickly along the financial stepping stool. A more current working class which was the quick recipient of the stream down market economy extended in size incredibly and immediately lost all its developmental devotions to communist developments and thoughts. The standard Left gatherings which had surrendered their space to pseudo-communist powers during TN's pre-advancement period, by mid 2000s had nearly been totally extracted from the political talk of the state which was presently progressively being directed by the new, optimistic, cosmopolitan working class that incidentally valued its in vogue 'political ignorance'.

The disentangling of the standard Left in Tamilnadu (and surprisingly in Andhra) had a lot of reasons. Initially, the Left gatherings were immensely subject to pitiful gifts and commitments from its party unit, patrons and ordinary citizens for their everyday hierarchical use. As the size of the political decision market developed with time its opponent gatherings had the option to round up millions from their rich supporters and degenerate practices while being in influence. Consequently the perpetually penurious Communists sensibly had no potential for success against their money rich adversaries who were just very glad to co-pick them into their brief electing coalitions. Furthermore, the Left gatherings couldn't track down available resources to sharpen their own association laborers and workers on class issues and proposition enduring answers for their everyday issues. Therefore, even individuals having a place with the Left wing worker's guilds minded less to decide in favor of the party during the races, utilizing their coordinated strength exclusively to accomplish handy solutions for day by day issues inside and outside their working environment. Thirdly, in the time of progression, the unregulated economy had imbued something else altogether social point of view toward its kin where careerism, commercialization and an all inescapable dread of endurance effectively bested Independence-period ethics like optimism, penance, social mindfulness and moral displeasure. Likewise, the unexpected breakdown of the Soviet Union in 1991 confounded the philosophical center of the party who abruptly couldn't react satisfactorily to questions questioning the legitimacy of their establishing speculations. A frightfully perplexed party tip top buried in self-uncertainty like this one, probably thought that it is hard to pass their rich hypothetical legacy to their cutting edge who normally might have summoned no tendency to fiddle with them. A mentally insipid Left party ruins the general public it possesses as well as gets consequently, oblivious and philosophically bankrupt unit into its overlay who complete a self-supporting pattern of scholarly shortage and ceaseless information drought.

Kerala, Soviet Union's last relic:

However, Kerala attributable to its totally extraordinary financial history went through an amazingly unique political excursion from that of its adjoining Tamilnadu. The early coming of Christian evangelists into Kerala, the quick change of Hindu lower positions into Christianity and Islam, fast spread of training through preacher claimed schools, outrageous persecution of lower rank laborers by their upper standing property managers and other critical variables dug the dirt for the growing of assailant insurrection developments drove by Soviet propelled Communists all over Kerala. Socialists endured the worst part of the overabundances released via property manager police nexus previously, then after the fact freedom which luckily gave them an incredible appointive benefit over that of their adversaries. Kerala was the first state in Quite a while to decide in favor of a non-Congress government in 1957 and the state gained extraordinary headway in wellbeing, instruction and sterilization indices.

ommunists assumed a huge part in extending of majority rules system in Kerala by engaging panchayati establishments and neighborhood urban bodies. Horticultural and modern cooperatives energized by the State brought laborers and ranchers together in incredible numbers cutting across unbending rank and strict divisions. Execution of government plans were initiated by party framework and nearby masses which assumed an incredible part in viably uncovering administrative and political defilement. Kerala turned into the primary state to accomplish 100% proficiency in the nation and furthermore stays the main state in India to have a greater number of females than males.

However such an environment where the majority assumed a functioning part in political undertakings, was not viewed as appropriate for industry by financial backers when India moved towards a market economy in 1991.

Kerala's economy it should be conceded was significantly subject to its huge diaspora housed in the distant Gulf notwithstanding deliberate endeavors by the State to assemble solid co-usable and public area businesses. Without legitimate administrative independence, no administration could seek to make a confident state economy in a different country like India. State legislatures, just like the case with the remainder of India need to continue to interest the Center for reserves on numerous occasions and consequently assembling a modern economy without the cooperation of the nearby private area by the State government is near impossible.

In the present situation, on one hand, a youthful and a yearning metropolitan working class in Kerala instructed by an intensely managed supportive of helpless state training framework, and one that was weaned on huge settlements from the Gulf gradually floats towards an amazing Hindu Right that arises on the guarantee of lucrative positions, breathtaking shopping centers and gated networks through market-driven monetary strategies. While on the other, the lower classes continue to lean toward the customary government assistance economy worked by Left and neighborhood Congress legislatures in political race after election.

However, Kerala stays the main state in India which keeps on evading the cross country pattern in a larger number of ways than one. It continues to record the most elevated levels of Human Development markers in India year on year rivaling the incomparable Industrial West on practically every one of them. On a comparative note, it is the main spot in India which actually holds the thoughts of Marx and Lenin near its heart even following 27 years of the breakdown of the Soviet Union, at an inquisitive time when the remainder of the nation is quick unmooring itself from its altruistic legacy.

HAPTER XIII

astern Promises

India's political economy was set apart to head leftward even before its introduction to the world. The scars of English Imperialism were new and rotting and the

Congress think tank drove by the visionary legislator, Jawaharlal Nehru had no other decision except for to go communist. The options given by the adjoining USSR were too enticing to even consider opposing - by mid 1950s the Soviet domain had restored breathtakingly inspite of the overwhelming impacts of the Second World War. Arranged economy and a favorable to helpless government assistance model summed up Nehru's vision for India and he set out toward that path notwithstanding powers pulling him from behind and sideways.

The Communist Party of India by 1948 had required an equipped rebellion against the 'middle class' government drove by Nehru and he reacted very much like each and every other public pioneer would do when confronted with vicious inner commotion - sending enormous scope suppression. He was helped on this count immensely by Sardar Patel whose hatred for left wingers was broadly known. The CPI, incapable to withstand serious state counter, was in a real sense devastated inside a couple of months principally because of absence of famous help combined with helpless comprehension of Indian conditions. The misfortune supported by the left was exceptionally enormous which thus reflected in the impending decisions. The majority too felt unsettled and the blowing up of their furnished strategies drained all their progressive vigor.Still, the party stayed the second biggest political outfit in India even in the wake of losing an immense lump of its unit to administrative repression.

Communists brace for a split:

Jawaharlal Nehru underscored the job of the State in dealing with the undertakings of the public economy and his administration set off to set up a ton of public area businesses whose commitment to country building turned significant in the forthcoming many years. Farming was given prime significance in the debut long term plans and India's agrarian creation multiplied and trebled during the 1960s. The modern result likewise developed complex which thus prodded an amazing restoration of the Indian economy interestingly post-Independence. Expectations for everyday comforts of Indians likewise rose because of which inquiries concerning public solidarity and social union post freedom were settled. Secularism was immovably bored into the personalities of Indians and public decisions demonstrated on numerous occasions that a larger part of Indians distinguished themselves solidly with the possibility of India regardless of racial and phonetic differences.

The Communists also were dazzled by the advancement India was making, directed by communist standards and Leninist standards of financial preparation while, in equal, frustration spread among a couple of left wing bunches whose

dream of a total communist upset was quickly blurring. These gatherings were not exactly off-base when they saw that the Congress, inspite of Nehru's endeavors was progressively succumbing to the plans of India's traditionalist classes and acting all things considered against the desire of the helpless larger part. Countless Congress officials and parliamentarians hailed from the rich upper positions and gave it their best shot to impede Nehru's driven land change program. Accordingly, land changes all over India were just barely fruitful and in country regions, abundance conveyance kept on being slanted for the customary elites. Pressures stewed among landowners and lower standing laborers even into the 1960s since administrative endeavors to work on the existences of the last option were not bearing much fruit.

Communists divide yet rule:

Nehru's weighty approach of worldwide non-arrangement was a huge achievement all around the Third world. The relationship of China, India's socialist neighbor with its ancestor, the USSR was souring consistently while Chinese pioneer Zhou En Lai joined Nehru at the Bandung Conference in 1955. China and India had frivolous boundary questions since the time the introduction of the republics however Nehru's enemy of American demeanor which showed in his endeavors to get China a long-lasting seat in the United Nations helped in limiting pressures for some time. The USSR was additionally intrigued with India's hostility towards the West and assisted the juvenile country with monstrous financial and specialized help. In its conflicts with Pakistan, the USSR undauntedly upheld India in different global discussions and helped it militarily. However, in 1962, China staggered Nehru by intersection the wilderness and assaulting Indian stations. It is accounted for that Nehru was not educated as expected with regards to the crumbling circumstance in the Aksai-Chin line and that his unreasonable dependence on Chinese altruism was liable for helpless Indian arrangements against the abrupt Chinese attack. The contention kept going near a month and India needed to surrender a piece of the contested region to the Chinese.

The effect of the Indo-Chinese clash was felt no place as vigorously as on the positions of the Communist Party. A group of the party since the time Independence had consistently taken a more harmless perspective on the Congress and hosted confided in the stupendous old gathering in its capacity to take India a communist way. Truth be told, the party sent a couple of its ideologues to penetrate the Congress echelons and clandestinely impact policymaking. This group upheld India

during the Indo-China war while the remainder of the party faltered in its position. The last option in under two years split away from the parent association shaping the colossally persuasive Communist Party of India (Marxist) in 1964. The new party was considered to have more grounded and more extreme pioneers than its parent and its impact spread all over West

Bengal. During the times of Siddharth Shankar Ray's main ministership in West Bengal (1972-77), Marxist aggressors and activists multiplied all around the rustic horticultural areas attempting to free the laborers from the overabundances of landowners. Beam following Patel's techniques in controling socialist rebellion enjoyed outrageous strategies for suppression that handily violated the limits of lawfulness. Huge number of socialists, honest laborers and ranch laborers were captured, attacked and killed during Indira Gandhi's crisis (1975-77).

However, Ray's strategies blew up when the Left Front cleared the gathering surveys in 1977. Bengal inside a couple of years showed the way for the remainder of the country on execution of the land change program and Jyoti Basu's endeavors as Chief Minister in breaking the authority of medieval property managers over the customarily mistreated laborers and laborers prevailed upon applauses from activists all India.

Relative Tranquility (1977-2008):

After CPI(M's) triumph in West Bengal in 1977, the Indian standard Left, it could securely be expressed, accomplished a time of relative soundness in their fortunes for the following thirty years or something like that. Naxalism then again, which began in the last part of the 1960s because of CPI(M's) split with its extreme Leninist kin was bound to amazingly in reverse provincial regions in West Bengal, Andhra Pradesh and Bihar. Anyway in practically no time, the Left had shockingly fostered a simple relationship with appointive governmental issues and their incessant collusions with middle class parties showed up more catalyst than really dreamer. The radicalism of the mid 1920s as well, was quick vanishing even among the Communist tip top and embitterment inside both the left gatherings continued to surface over and over through expanding splinter gatherings and ousted erudite people. The Left gatherings nonetheless, had the option to get at least 40 seats in the Lok Sabha during each ensuing general political race which gave them generous influence as for strategy making and execution. The various worker's guilds and laborer social orders, under the immense Communist umbrella helped a great deal during this period attributable to significant left-wing presence in the Parliament.

Indira Gandhi's development as the most remarkable innovator in the post-Nehruvian time kept on giving desires to the endurance of communism in Indian approach making. The abrogation of privy satchels and nationalization of banks in the last part of the 1960s, the two of which critical advances the communist way drew the adoration of the Left gatherings.

Indira consistently guaranteed that her political way of talking transformed effectively into a legendary fight between the left and the right-she addressing the supportive of helpless Good and her rivals having a place with the counter helpless fiendish camp. Anyway she was amazingly cautious as not to permit the battle to explode into a full-scale class struggle and subsequently utilized the Emergency as a way to dull the edges of both the right and left wing components in the country. Her surprising death in 1984 denoted a huge turnaround toward Indian political economy. As the remainder of the world affected by Reagan-Thatcherite thoughts was unmooring itself from government assistance inheritances roused by Keynesianism, India too created utilization of the open door of Indira's destruction to move towards the right. Rajiv Gandhi and ensuing heads of the Congress, directed occasionally by balancing powers of left-wing worker's guilds and mass associations cleared the ground for monetary progression in 1991.

look into the organs and diaries of the left gatherings that were distributed during this period offers shocking forecasts on the future effect on India's nation and the approaching repercussions of its move towards financial advancement. The Left gatherings had kept on notice as ahead of schedule as during the 1990s, about a potential breakdown of India's agrarian area in case of a change driven State pulling out itself from the market. Alerts about unreasonable degrees of financial disparity, unmanageable degrees of wrongdoing subsequently, corporate loot of India's regular assets and irreversible estrangement of Adivasis and tribals from their customary natural surroundings, potential outcomes of aggravations from Islamist-Wahabbist furnished gatherings in case of India's hug of Hindutva patriot thoughts, risks of getting entrapped into the tacky trap of global economy all of that which sound frightfully judicious today show up all over left-wing diaries and organs during this period. Calls for activity against dark cash reserved in assessment shelters abroad and their injurious consequences for Indian economy can be found in press explanations gave by left wing pioneers as ahead of schedule as in the 1990s.

eft wing legislatures in Bengal, Kerala and Tripura kept on carrying out government assistance plans in their separate states even after India's hug of neoliberalism. Tripura, under the Left Front Government for close

to 25 years took incredible steps like Kerala as far as training and wellbeing. It turned into the primary state in the North-East to dispose of the draconian AFSPA law whose nullification was a sign of political dependability produced by the debilitating of nearby hardliner and secessionist powers. In the 2004 general races, the Left gatherings recorded their most elevated count in the Lok Sabha and made a post survey collusion with the Congress - drove UPA to keep the Hindu-patriot BJP out of force. They were instrumental in achieving the greatest leader program in neoliberal India, the National Rural Employment Guarantee program which guaranteed at least 100 days of work in rustic regions. Their impact additionally altogether dialed back the change situated UPA government's endeavors to offer public area organizations to private substances and furthermore assumed a significant part in holding rising petroleum costs within proper limits.

You Reform, You Die:

The Left Front Government in West Bengal by late 2000s was drawing tremendous fire from different quarters for not having supported a business-accommodating environment in the State even subsequent to being in power for near thirty years. The analysis at first was not treated in a serious way by Jyoti Basu when he was in power however his replacement, a maddened Buddhadeb Bhattacharya needed to react in an unexpected way. He welcomed the Tatas to put resources into Bengal and guaranteed backing to them in issues of land obtaining. The Bengal ranchers the majority of whom were recipients of Basu's property change were not exactly open to the public authority's thought. They opposed land obtaining egged on by provincial Maoist and other resistance powers making incredible embarassment the 'transformed' Communist administration. Befuddled with respect to how to react to public clamor against its favorable to business gauges, the Left Front Government smothered public fomentation savagely in 2007. Inside a territory whose individuals were known for their antagonism towards enormous business houses and corporate business visionaries, an inquisitive disposition which was planted and developed by the officeholder government itself for over thirty years, this transition to viciously smother genuine difference ended up to be meaningless not exactly political self destruction. In the 2009 general decisions, following the UPA-Left separation in the Center on the disagreeable Indo-US atomic arrangement, the Left gatherings experienced a significant appointive inversion in West Bengal. Their count, thus contracted to 29 in the Lok Sabha, their least ever in post-Nehruvian India. In the resulting get together and general races, the Left experienced huge misfortunes in Bengal and over the most recent ten years or something like that, their stunning destruction from

Bengal's memory has all the earmarks of being practically finished. Having been not able to grow past their restricted boondocks, the Left gatherings have been minimized viably from India's appointive field and along these lines from the country's political talk as well.

cut above the rest:

The purposes behind the Left's decrease are very self-evident and have been adequately examined in the past part. Here I might want to examine the tradition of the Left in India which has generally either been ceaselessly distorted or terribly underreported. The Left development, it should be noted, assumed a key part in India's opportunity battle and forfeited a large number of its majority to the reason. All over provincial India, they were the principal individuals to speak loudly against exceptionally old authority of the upper positions and conventional elites over poor people and oppressed. They assumed an irreplaceable part in the developing of majority rule government in a primitive, hardship torn, in reverse India and in engendering the upsides of European edification like secularism, free discourse and social fairness among the masses.

ost-Independence, their furnished just as tranquil battles against neighborhood elites and industrialists guaranteed that the laborers and laborers had the option to work on their functioning conditions and ways of life essentially. Their mass associations delivered both uneducated and helpless ladies from the common laborers and permitted them to involve top authority and authoritative posts. In both Bengal and Kerala, panchayati raj organizations got a significant lift under Left guideline because of which ladies were addressed enough in nearby bodies. Above all, the Communists' part in safeguarding India's common personality in the midst of successive public conflicts and consistently rising character legislative issues can't be overstated.

Having gone through near 70 years both at the heart and fringe of India's constituent nation, the Left actually protects the differentiation of being the main standard political outfit in the nation to stay untainted by outrages or political debasement. A large portion of the heads of the Left have remained paragons of individual goodness, driving basic and sacrificial lives. Moreover, it can securely be said that the quantity of savvy people, academicians and researchers in the Communist crew alone may effectively dwarf those having a place with rest of the relative multitude of ideological groups set up. The way that both Bengal and Kerala produce the best works in different social and imaginative disciplines and the profound entrenchment of socialism in the socio-social scene of both the states are not simple coincidences.

In the present neoliberal India, the campaign of the Communists against class and rank double-dealing are not finished at this point. In the slopes and backwoods of profound inside Chattisgarh, where the Indian Army agreeing with the state-supported fear based oppressor outfit Salwa Judum take on a great many poor and landless tribals and Adivasis to pursue them away from their customary environments for tremendous mining partnerships peering toward India's biggest stores of bauxite and minerals, it is the Communist assailants (Maoists) who are at the cutting edge of the battle working indefatigably to reestablish the land to whom it legitimately has a place. As writer Jeyamohan writes in his blog, no other party or development is as devoted and focused on the reason for poor people and oppressed as the Left in India. Anything that might be their imperfections, strategic disappointments and chronicled botches, it's anything but a distortion to say that in the midst of the huge number of gatherings mushrooming to a great extent in India's vote based country occasionally, there are really just two kinds of political associations in India - the Left and the rest.

THE WITHERING AWAY OF THE STATE

CHAPTER XIV

What did the Soviet Union mean?

When the USSR was made in 1922 there could be no vagueness concerning how the residents felt about it. The majority of the laborers, laborers and craftsmans were enchanted at being essential for a notable civilizational advance, something different countries were not fit for doing. A larger part of them expected better lives and a climate brimming with guarantee and positive thinking about the future invaded all through the domain. Lenin anyway was more a commonsense man than a heartfelt visionary, who continued to underline the hugeness of the impediments set up towards their walk to communism. He continued to let individuals know that they might need to make tremendous forfeits basically in the present moment to rework the current creation relations as to accomplish a sensible proportion of libertarianism. Furthermore individuals were prepared to work for him as millions enlisted in the Red Army to serve their freshly discovered Fatherland during the quick Civil War. Indeed, even after Lenin requested the brief withdrawal of individual flexibilities placing some sort of a military law set up, there wasn't a lot of discontent or aggregate opposition at first. Before long Stalin's landing in the scene, the existences of normal Russians, it should be conceded was quick abandoning awful to worse.

From the last part of the 1930s to the start of the World War ll, Russians lost more than they acquired overall new dictatorial request at the top which guaranteed public steadiness and inner harmony tracked down articulation. The new request had in a couple of years turned strong and intractable and it can't be rejected that most Russians were seen as wavering between sensations of devotion to their merciless system and those of disappointment at the demanding requests and forfeits it commanded from the conventional residents. As the realm entered the War, Stalin's enticement for the majority to shield their country from the hostility of the foe was joined by unwinding of limitations in individual flexibilities and privileges. Russia's misfortunes in the War were humongous and practically all progressive energy of the majority had been depleted toward its finish. Notwithstanding, Russia's triumph in the conflict was amazing regardless of whether it was pyrrhic and Stalin attempted to gain by this accomplishment to restore the country's hanging soul. The nation was starting over from the beginning as far as financial principles as well as in those of individual flexibilities and basic freedoms. One more dazzling restoration of economy was accomplished under a withering yet still colossally alluring Stalin by which time individuals had become acclimated to the Stalinist request, which was very like their days under the Tsars.

Khrushchev's time was a period when the normal Russian was finally conceded the opportunity to inhale simple and a comparable situation followed under an innocuous Brezhnev. By the center of Brezhnev's rule, Russia had changed to the point of being indistinguishable from a medieval, semi-modern in reverse country not exactly recognizable from an Asiatic government into an advanced, modern power which could talk in equivalent terms with the Western superpowers. The ways of life under the Bolsheviks were customary contrasted with the West however obviously superior to those under the Tsars. A large number of workers and craftsmans and workers approached free and mandatory training, sensible medical services and disinfection. The exceptionally old subjugation to land and crude characters had been hopelessly broken and most Russians had changed themselves into agents, engineers, modern laborers, educators, and so forth Despite the fact that Russia was still less free contrasted with its Western rivals, the reliability of the residents to the foundation was at this point very certain. This is a method of flattening a gigantic and unmerited falsehood cultivated and supported by a misleading and a hopelessly threatening Western entrepreneur media that practically all Russian residents detested the Bolsheviks and were holding on to break into a new, lavish and progressed life that advanced free enterprise clearly could provide.

An incredible story of contradictions:

As a considerable lot of you would have noticed, the reason for this series isn't either

to legitimize how the Communists helped and outside Russia or to expose the million fantasies that they apportioned unjustifiably about the province of USSR's inside issues every so often. What's more, I have no expectation to flaunt my capacity to give a decent judgment about the Soviet Empire because of the tremendous subjectivity associated with this discussion. As referenced before, my endeavor to return to the tale of the Bolshevik Empire developed exclusively out of a profound interest by virtue of its extraordinary peculiarity of character whose imperfections and accomplishments challenge each other vivaciously in extent in pretty much each and every component of it.

SSR was the primary state on the planet to owe loyalty to the great principles of Marxism and subsequently it is sensible for any understudy of history to anticipate a pinch of balance, opportunity and freedom to carry on with a decent life in such an avowedly 'idealistic' climate. In any case, shockingly, USSR came not even close to it. The Empire reduced every current opportunity, expanded death camps and standardized them, seized property, crushed difference, legitimized starvations and their misusing. Exactly when we smell the shades of a religious state or one of a Fascist kind in its previously mentioned attributes, out of nowhere, an entirely new moderate aspect is uncovered to us. Russia was the primary country on the planet to build up 'full work' something the industrialist countries just didn't have the ability to accomplish. The Tsarist Russian culture of the 1900s had barely anything to do with that of the 1960s with practically all of the general population very much settled in into present day foundations of political economy, a change which required hundreds of years for the Europeans to accomplish. The USSR, it can't be denied was the main nation to accomplish one more incredible progressive achievement, in particular the freedom of ladies, something which is as yet a pipedream in numerous as far as anyone knows moderate countries. The Bolsheviks were quick to present maternity leave, legitimize separate and accommodate equivalent compensation for ladies with men. Crèches had large amounts of Soviet Russia and female investment in work was a remarkable standard than exception.

As antiquarian Isaac Deutscher notes in his book, the Stalinist organization acquired every one of the medieval qualities of Tsarist Russia however, by giving its residents formal and expert instruction alongside

necessary examinations in Marxism, it accidentally planted the seeds for its own destruction. Present day antiquarians tend to look at and liken 20thcentury despots like
Stalin and Hitler to decry the previous eagerly with a secret intention to subvert the allure of Communism out and out. Notwithstanding, one

necessities to surrender that the extent of Stalin's wrongdoings against mankind can't be viewed as lesser or inconsequential in correlation with that of Hitler. Stalin arises a preferred leader over Hitler provided that we think about different aspects of his organization. Hitler's administration flourished to a great extent on bigoted scorn, spread and intensified it with the end goal of making a profoundly divided society to the place of super durable irreversibility. Stalin's system then again worked with a resolute effectiveness to push the general public the exceptionally inverse way towards destroying every single crude character and divisions and making a for all time bound together entirety. Obviously, Hitler's separating mission bombed before long it took off while Stalin's main goal was a stupendous achievement which might have been even more magnificent had it been accomplished without shedding human blood and gobbling up the existences of millions of innocents.

It is additionally frequently contended by numerous erudite people that Hitler prevailed with regards to changing a frail and crippled Germany into an amazing, modern country inside a range of under 10 years accordingly giving huge number of occupations to its ruined labor force, something which his archetypes couldn't accomplish. By misrepresenting the adventures of Hitler, there is frequently a deceptive endeavor to deprecate the communist accomplishments of the USSR. It merits emphasizing the way that Germany was the most industrialized country in Europe
even before the start of the 20thcentury. Indeed, even Marx and his devotees including Lenin unequivocally accepted that Germany will be the main country on the planet to go communist given the enormous modern headway it had made during the modern unrest. So when Hitler took the country over in 1933, he was just further developing what was at that point there in Germany in complete differentiation to the regressive territory of Soviet Russia. Additionally Germany's modern improvement depended to a great extent on the deadly implement industry whose working was thusly absolutely reliant upon the possibilities of Germany's conflict making capacities. A great deal of market analysts settle on the way that Germany's striking financial advancement owed a ton to Hitler's central goal to finish his

retribution on its adversaries who constrained the Versailles' deal down its throat. Nazi Germany made due on what was known as a War Economy which would have imploded totally during peacetime.

onversely, Stalinist Russia inside under 10 years was giving indications of contending with cutting edge modern countries including the United States. Exactly when its possibilities were looking into, the USSR was pushed into one of the most crushing struggles in mankind's set of experiences. The USSR persevered through a massive human and monetary calamity over the span of the conflict and inside 10 years subsequent to winning it, coordinated a blending resurgence under Stalin's authority to find its Western opponents. Any liberal antiquarian of the 20th century would consent to the way that no other country on the planet might have supported such huge monetary inversions, stay unaffected and display such uncanny strength to reestablish itself to business as usual. During Khrushchev's period during the 1960s, the modern result of the USSR was quick finding that of the United States.

However, the more we will quite often credit these accomplishments to Stalin, we all the while neglect to recognize the Russian ordinary citizen on whose soul and penance the whole communist building stood gladly for over forty years after the conflict. What's more it is likewise ludicrous to contend that the Russians battled for their Fatherland, gave their lives eagerly and worked energetically to assemble communism exclusively because of pressure and state constraint. Various records including the new book by Svetlana Alexevitch gives confirmations of how dedicated Soviet Russians were to the reason for their country and towards building communism. In different spots of the book, Svetlana draws out the obvious contrasts in disposition between past Soviet residents and those of today. The residents of the present industrialist Russia are taunted continually by their archetypes who lived under communism for having fortified themselves to modest things like professions and items for their endurance. War veterans and educators and modern laborers under Soviet Russia gladly gloat about living for an 'ideal' (communism) criticizing the situation under the new entrepreneur order.

Svetlana's record adds weight to different suspicions that rotate around the present old Russians, a greater part of whom have a 'nostalgic outlook on the Soviet Union. Those, whom Svetlana talked with, one can notice, vent their disappointment of having been sold out by the people who vouched and lobbied for the destroying of Soviet Russia in guarantee of opportunity and majority rules system. Most Soviet Russians unequivocally trusted that with the appearance of perestroika and glasnost, there would be more press opportunity, an expanded cooperation of residents in the organization of the state and steady facilitating of standards as for their communication with the 'outside'. Be that as it may, what occurred inside not exactly a large portion of 10 years was the foundation of a totally outsider unregulated economy constrained by neighborhood and unfamiliar personal stakes in conspiracy with new oligarchs set on plundering Russia and its satellites. Russian residents who were accustomed to approaching free education,

medical care and modest lodging with 'respectable' work under communism were abruptly approached to rush and join the race for saving their livelihoods. They were requested to adjust promptly to the prerequisites from the all-new free enterprise request, master new abilities including misleading and trick and look into the new standards of until now obscure 'rodent race'.

Making sense of the Soviet Experiment:

Just before I trust the evidence speak for itself, I wish to give a legit and succinct record of what I for one all in, about the peculiar story of the Soviet Union. Exactly when I was acquainted with the peculiarity of the Soviet Union in my youth through the kaleidoscope of Communist promulgation with the assistance of my dad, I was profoundly fascinated of its accomplishments and guarantees. As a long time elapsed, I learned through industrialist media and its proselytizers about the frightful violations that had been submitted inside the Empire. Truly I was shocked and the more I learned of them from the perspectives of different intelligent people and antiquarians, all I felt was an internal repugnance against the Communists and their indecent nature for creating untruths and lies. This was the time I was additionally allowed into perusing Marxist texts and the hypothetical establishments of communism. Obviously, the hypothetical adequacy of the Marxist standards and its capacity to dispassionately scrutinize the peculiarity of private enterprise entranced me. At this point, my repugnance for the Communists and their promulgation organs had been somewhat mellowed however something about the immense hole between their hypothesis and practice kept me both captivated and horrified. My interest developed when I began concentrating on Russian history from sources having a place with different schools of political idea and the hostile inconsistencies I noted according to different points of view just wound up honing my fixation on the account of Soviet Russia.

So how would I sort out it? Allow me to put my realities front and center.

Soviet Russia killed its very own large number residents. The Communist Party ate its very own large number devoted unit. For what one may inquire? Did the Soviet chiefs gather enormous fortunes from the works and blood of conventional Russians? No. Or on the other hand atleast did they accomplish Socialism? Well not actually. They approached. Gracious, does it matter one may inquire. Communism at the expense of millions of lives? Indeed it truly doesn't make any difference. Assuming Socialism can be accomplished distinctly through the butcher and evacuating of millions of lives, let us say a resonating No to Socialism. However, is Socialism just that? Killing millions, mingling destitution, dispossessing individual flexibility and property? Absolutely no. Then, at that point, what do we conclude

about it? Do we acknowledge it or reject it?

small humanist hiding underneath the essayist in me shakes and falls down at the loathsomeness of what occurred in the Soviet Union under Stalin. Had I been allowed an opportunity to live under such conditions I would most likely have selected myself out. In any case, when I go through the record of what you call the Free Market which is frequently promoted to be the option for communism, all I get isn't anything not exactly the notorious chill down my spine. Assuming you don't really accept that me, generously leaf through the accounts of Latin America and Africa regarding how private enterprise butchered and oppressed huge number of honest residents for the sake of progress and advancement over the most recent couple of hundreds of years. On the off chance that you don't have time, generously read about books on our own insight under the opportunity adoring Brits.

o here is my end explanation. Communism killed a large number of living souls in the USSR savagely. During Stalin's system, the public authority was one colossal unstoppable dispensing with machine. In any case, whenever you are finished contracting at the frightfulness of what occurred out there, open your shut eyes. Illuminate yourself to the way that Socialism likewise saved a great many lives across the globe simultaneously from the attacks of settler free enterprise. It gave desires to huge numbers of working masses and assisted them with battling their noble battle against ruthless private enterprise. Indeed, even today, things we underestimate like legitimately ensured working hours, benefits, fortunate asset, maternity leave, casting a ballot rights, the option to sort out, the right to training, food and a nice living owe their starting points to the possibility of Socialism. The USSR paying little mind to how close it came to accomplishing Socialism inside, was seen all around the world by the decision classes as nothing under a living exemplification of Socialism, a thought that basically alarmed them. It was that dread, that awful dread to shield themselves from the authority of the average workers that Socialism represented, that constrained them to allow every one of the privileges and opportunities that you appreciate today. Let that sink in.

CHAPTER XV

he Implosion

he Treaty of 1922 on the Creation of the USSR was finished up by the tops of the Russian, Ukrainian, Byelorussian and Transcaucasian Republics on 30 December that very year. The republics met up because of the colonialist risks presented by Western entrepreneur powers to weaken communism as shown by the first four-year long Civil War. In 1940, the USSR filled in size to oblige eleven additional republics including those of the Baltic States. This large number of nations were constitutionally given the option to join and withdraw from the Union at will.

he 1936 Constitution of the Soviet Union perceived the main job of the Communist Party of the Soviet Union in the organization of the Empire.

The Good Samaritan:

Gorbachev in 1986 transparently disavowed the Brezhnev Doctrine. This demonstration joined with glasnost and perestroika changed the substance of the USSR in practically no time. The changes were two dimensional-the two political and monetary. The last option implied expanded independence for state-possessed divisions which included remittance for common collaboration between themselves, unwinding of creation targets set by Central policymakers, making of co-usable social orders following Tito's Yugoslavian model, unionization of the labor force to work with aggregate haggling, motivation based compensation framework to build usefulness and some additional changing measures the vast majority of which were basically not piece of the Soviet framework since its initiation. These plans to resuscitate the economy to fulfill expanded need for buyer products looked judicious however very inadequate. It should likewise be noticed that Gorbachev, as he is regularly seen to be was not a 'free marketeer' but rather a communist reformer profoundly dedicated towards bettering the existences of his residents. The financial change grew a ton of naysayers inside the party who feared a takeoff from the Marxist standards of 'arranged economy' however soon they were supplanted by Gorbachev with the people who toed his line obediently.

But the most youthful Head of the Soviet State couldn't be confused with his monetary change which was a decent positive development regardless of whether it had a lot of impediments. It was just his extreme work to 'politically' change the Union that wound up meaning something bad for the Revolution and its establishing thoughts. His political change called for more prominent straightforwardness and responsibility which were essentially an abomination to a significant number of the party managers and officials. His way breaking work to permit analysis inside the Union and to open the ears of the country to outside prompted unanticipated results. Interestingly, autonomous presses jumped up all around the Union and unfamiliar media were permitted to answer to and outside the Union. This move had profoundly subverted the state publicity talk which had effectively for a really long time kept up with the extraordinary deception that the Union was showing improvement over the remainder of the world in practically all files. News channels before long began revealing the tricks and trickeries of the neighborhood administrators and permitted pundits to utilize their foundation to voice disagree which included uncovering the grave wrongdoings carried out by the Union's previous chiefs and the awful concealments that followed. This was verifiably an extraordinary shock for the normal Russian whose enthusiasm to his Fatherland was profoundly connected to good conclusions about his notorious chiefs. Add to this the way of life shock suffered by the Russians because of unfamiliar TV which described accounts of Westerners living substantially more rich and more liberated lives than their own. Yet, that was not the most exceedingly terrible of all.

Moscow's unexpected shift towards a liberal demeanor befuddled the party chiefs in different pieces of the Union. Ukraine, Armenia, Azerbaijan were for such an extremely long time been remote constrained by Moscow however the authorities of these nations observed their hands unexpectedly unwound by Gorbachev's change. The since quite a while ago denied the right to speak freely of discourse and the option to contradict reinforced the patriot components in these nations which started to make their bid for power taking on a feeble neighborhood Communist initiative which had no assistance from Moscow out of nowhere. Gorbachev was informed about these unanticipated turns of events and he emphatically would not put forth attempts towards shortening their force. The youthful pioneer, assuming that anything was just strolling his discussion and acting like a genuine communist. The Soviet constitution had perceived the republics' on the right track to withdraw from the Union and soon it was passed on to the heads of these nations to deal with rising patriot feelings. Inside a little while, the greater constituents of the Union were either straightforwardly offering for autonomy from Moscow or attempting to mount lively obstruction against the nearby enemy of change Communist leadership.

he Union goes to polls:

Gorbachev's sights on international strategy were clear and unobstructed by the deeds of his archetypes. The Oil shock experienced by the Union in 1985 had injured the economy and provoked Russian withdrawal from Afghanistan. The Moscow chief had chosen not exclusively to de-heighten pressures with its archrival in Washington yet additionally to hit an arrangement with them regardless of the expense it involved. The greater part of his endeavors towards demilitarization were one-sided and soon Reagan's replacement George Bush of the US was stunned by Gorbachev's responsibility towards harmony and kinship. He dazzled the West extraordinarily when he let go of East Germany in 1989 permitting the Berlin Wall to fall flagging the finish of the fifty-year old Cold War with the US. This assisted Gorbachev with grounding the Red Army extensively and redirect the assets reserved for military costs towards expanding modern productivity.

But from the start of 1989, Gorbachev gradually started to perceive the results that followed his choice to open up the Union. The counter change camp inside the CPSU did their best to hinder him however Gorbachev opposed them with fresher thoughts. He in 1989 debilitated the Politburo by carrying the party to elastic stamp his proposition for the making of another Congress of People's Deputies. The Congress should house 2250 delegates chose through direct surveys who were thus permitted to choose the Supreme Soviet headed by the new President. The Union went to races in March 1989 and Gorbachev's camp won an enormous triumph disregarding individuals' declining confidence in him making him the main President of the USSR (that included Russia and fourteen other republics).

Even however Gorbachev's endeavors towards democratizing the Union looked praiseworthy, different observers from across the world were blaming him for entrusting himself with such countless powers as the President the USSR accordingly sabotaging different organs of the party. This allegation genuine examines the substance of such a lot of proof where the new President was found either headstrong or unrepentant over the repercussions of his change. He neglected to accept exhortation from old, yet reasonable hardliners who supported change in a painstakingly arranged and staged way. He would not pay attention to the counter change camp even on genuine issues, for example, the malicious impacts his change had made on the economy. His enemy of liquor drive which brought about enormous income misfortunes had harmed the financial wellbeing of the Union and made a gigantic underground market for stash soul. The State couldn't uphold financed food items due to declining incomes and consequently costs rose which thus was not joined by relating wage modifications. Strikes broke across different pieces of the Union which were taken advantage of as far as possible by contradicting patriot components. Numerous business analysts, by and large lambast the lacks of Gorbachev's lively monetary plan for having floated away from the standards of financial preparation without satisfactorily establishing the frameworks for another option, useful, market-communist structure well ahead of time, something which China formulated viably. Thus the monetary change didn't really matter procuring the fury of both moderate and reformist components inside the party.

In October 1989, the recently made Supreme Soviet casted a ballot to eliminate held seats for the CPSU in public and neighborhood decisions naming the reservations as completely 'undemocratic'. It was a memorable choice that abused the Soviet Constitution which underlined the main job of the Communist

Party in the Union's organization. In December 1989, the Supreme Soviet casted a ballot for holding direct decisions in every one of the fifteen constituent republics much to the caution of Gorbachev.

The year 1989 was a characterizing year in Soviet history that saw a flood of patriot exhibitions and conflicts in its different constituent republics. Gorbachev at this point despite having won power through famous races started to give indications of ineptitude in dealing with these battles. He reacted some of the time through military and once in a while through appeasing means which sucked all open trust in him. The immediate decisions held in 1990 across the Union prompted the loss of the CPSU in Georgia, Armenia, Latvia, Lithuania, Moldova and Estonia which quickly picked the way of autonomy from the Union.

The USSR without Russia:

In 1985, Boris Yeltsin was welcomed by Gorbachev to assume control over the party capacities in the Russian capital. Yeltsin was chosen based on his reformist preferences and was before long enlisted into the Politburo for his work. However regularly called crude and chatty by numerous individuals of his partners, Boris was known for his heartbeat on the majority. He regularly exceeded his cutoff points by connecting with individuals all alone and his notoriety came in great stead for his speedy height to the top. It is known dependably that his own aspirations to drive were immediately divined by the VIP and his manipulative conduct came up for analysis frequently. The youthful Mayor of Moscow before long left his situation in the Politburo in 1987 after vigorously condemning Gorbachev straightforwardly at a Central Committee meeting.

Soon Yeltsin's daring discourse in the Central Committee chiding Gorbachev was printed and circled the nation over which did an extraordinary arrangement to set up him as a solid disorderly figure inside the CPSU who had the strange guts to stand up even to the Head of the State with regards to his residents' freedoms. Boris blamed Gorbachev for increasingly slow changes all the while censuring his imperious inclinations. In the mean time, laborer turmoil alongside serious deficiencies of food spread all around the Union. Boris benefited from the defiant wave and challenged Russia's free decisions in 1990. The recently chosen Congress of the People's agents of Russia decided in favor of Boris Yeltsin to head the Supreme Soviet of Russia in May that very year resisting Gorbachev's instructions.

The President of the USSR, Gorbachev from here on out needed to assume the Head of the Russian Republic, Boris Yeltsin-an errand which turned into all the

more troublesome because of ambiguities regarding partition of abilities between the President of the Union and the Head of the Russian State. To compound the situation for Gorbachev, Yeltsin in July 1990 left the CPSU in the party's 28thCongress finishing socialist imposing business model in Moscow.

However Gorbachev reacted by mooting holding a mandate all around the excess Soviet region over the subject of 'the protection of the USSR with full opportunity and freedoms to people, all things considered'. On March 12, 1991 a bigger number of than 80% of the residents took an interest in the mandate and near three-fourths decided in favor of the protection of the USSR and its communist type of government. This implied that residents dwelling in Russia, Ukraine, Byelorussia, Kazakhstan, Azerbaijan, Uzbekistan, Kirghizia, Turkmenistan and Tajikistan republics were agreeable to remaining inside the Union under communism. Be that as it may, a wily Yeltsin had figured out how to hold an equal mandate that very day on whether to make the post of President of Russia who could be straightforwardly chosen by individuals and consequently would appreciate advantages and opportunity unencumbered by the impacts of authoritative gatherings. Russians casted a ballot for it and direct races to the post of President of Russia were hung on June 12, 1991.

Gorbachev named Nikolai Ryzhov in the interest of the CPSU while Yeltsin challenged as a free. The falling fame of the Union's President was show in the political race results with Yeltsin surveying 58% of the vote beating CPSU's competitor by more than 43 rate focuses. In any case, it is to be noticed that Yeltsin's mission for the races was never commenced on a 'unrestricted economy' board and thus individuals lifted up him simply in light of the fact that they confused him with a submitted 'communist' reformer.

Yeltsin held onto the drive in a flash to remove Gorbachev and the CPSU from the Russian soil. Yeltsin's Russia pronounced itself autonomous from the Soviet Union following the outcomes came out.

Goodbye Lenin!

Russia's exit from the Soviet Union which was impending right from the first, delivered futile the reason for the actual Union. The other more modest republics had consented to be important for the Union just with the end goal of producing a nearby local co-activity with an amazing Russia at the middle that could complete one another in the midst of hardship. Gorbachev's fumble of the circumstance in the more modest republics and glaring ineffectualness of the nearby Communist authorities because of force mongering and infighting exacerbated circumstances in the provincial capitals and the most significant towns

of the Union.

frantic Gorbachev tried to rebuild the Union along less brought together lines by acquainting another Treaty with save it. Be that as it may, hardliners inside the CPSU abruptly declared a highly sensitive situation in August 1991 and requested the Red Army to capture Gorbachev at his dacha to reprove him for his 'hostile to Soviet exercises'. The upset was without a doubt coordinated without earlier planning and vision by the moderate group of the CPSU and neglected to energize public help. Yeltsin utilized the circumstance to censure the CPSU and its dictatorial ways and urged Russians to confront it. The overthrow imploded in under three days and Gorbachev was set free right away. The fresh insight about the bombed overthrow spread all around different republics and carried the distinction of the CPSU to a new low.

On December 1, 1991 taking cues from Russia, the second biggest republic of the Union, Ukraine casted a ballot for autonomy joining the long queue of withdrawing republics. Inside seven days, the heads of Russia, Ukraine and Byelorussia (Belarus) gathered at Minsk and marked the Belovezha Accord to formally affirm the death of the Union of Soviet Socialist Republics at 69 years old. The heads of different republics accumulated at Alma-Ata to officially break up the Union on December 21, 1991.

On Christmas day that very year, Mikhail Gorbachev in a broadcast address reported his acquiescence as President of the USSR from Kremlin. Exactly the same day, Russia embraced a resolution to rename itself from 'Russian Soviet Federative Socialist Republic' to 'Russian Federation' to state its separation from communism and the Union. After Gorbachev left the Kremlin, the Soviet Flag bearing the popular Hammer and Sickle was brought down and supplanted with a tricolor at Moscow.

Post Script

he extremely one week from now in 1992, Yeltsin let free a progression of market-situated financial changes called The Shock Therapy gave over by a gathering of business analysts flying in from the IMF for Russia.

By 1998, it was assessed that the GDP of Russia had fallen underneath half of what it had been in the climactic periods of the Soviet breakdown attributable to the presentation of Yeltsin's unregulated economy reforms.

n 2001, a report by business analyst Steven Rosefielde assessed that more than 3 million Russians kicked the bucket rashly somewhat recently by virtue of the aimless opening up of the Russian economy to outer market forces.

www.ingramcontent.com/pod-product-compliance
Lightning Source LLC
La Vergne TN
LVHW040909150826
845672LV00007B/1953

* 9 7 9 8 7 7 9 7 3 7 1 8 0 *